SUPERFOOD SNACKS

100 DELICIOUS, ENERGIZING &
NUTRIENT-DENSE RECIPES

SUPERFOOD SNACKS

JULIE MORRIS

bestselling author of *Superfood Smoothies* & *Superfood Juices*

STERLING
New York

STERLING
New York

An Imprint of Sterling Publishing
1166 Avenue of the Americas
New York, NY 10036

ISBN 978-1-4549-0558-5

Distributed in Canada by Sterling Publishing
c/o Canadian Manda Group, 664 Annette Street
Toronto, Ontario, Canada M6S 2C8
Distributed in the United Kingdom by GMC Distribution Services
Castle Place, 166 High Street, Lewes, East Sussex, England BN7 1XU
Distributed in Australia by Capricorn Link (Australia) Pty. Ltd.
P.O. Box 704, Windsor, NSW 2756, Australia

For information about custom editions, special sales, and premium and corporate purchases,
please contact Sterling Special Sales at 800-805-5489 or specialsales@sterlingpublishing.com.

Manufactured in Canada

2 4 6 8 10 9 7 5 3 1

www.sterlingpublishing.com

CONTENTS

"Let's make something!"

That was always the innocent statement that started it.

And, as usual, our resulting culinary predicament was completely accidental. Mustering all our nine-year-old wisdom and problem-solving abilities, my friend Katie and I, suited up nicely in our matching Rainbow Brite pajamas, were huddled inside my tiny closet, frantically trying to hide no less than twelve—yes, *twelve*—huge bags of freshly made popcorn underneath a pile of rumpled clothes. Personally, I was considering taking up permanent asylum in there.

"They'll never find it here," Katie whispered to me with earnest, large eyes, referring to my unsuspecting, now popcornless parents. We looked at each other for a moment with expectant fear before finally, simultaneously, bursting out in uncontrollable giggles. We had done it again—messed up a recipe to such unthinkably terrible heights that the only option was to get rid of the evidence as quickly as possible. And hide.

Katie was my very best friend throughout grade school. I like to think we were pretty good kids, but we had a long-standing reputation with our parents for wreaking havoc when we got together in the kitchen. And "The Popcorn Incident," as it is now officially referred to, was no different. All we had wanted to do was make popcorn balls—enough to feed our entire Girl Scout troop—but in the excitement of jumping in and making the popcorn *before* reading the recipe in full, we neglected to notice, until it was far too late, that we didn't have the other five (out of six) ingredients at my house. (I suppose it also bears mentioning that we later discovered we only needed two bags of popcorn, not twelve.)

The Popcorn Incident was one of many. There was the time Katie and I tried to bake gummy bears inside of brownies, which never got much farther than a pan of mush. Or the time we needed to melt chocolate for a frosting and enlisted the help of the microwave—setting it for way, way, *way* too long and learning the important lesson that microwaves cook significantly faster than their stove-top counterpart. That "lesson" turned our chocolate into blackened concrete, which adhered permanently to my mother's favorite bowl. "Let's make something," back then, was probably a little closer to a scientific experiment than a culinary endeavor.

Our catastrophes were primarily due to our continual habit of making "substitutions," or in other words our not-so-brilliant replacements for any needed ingredient we were unable to find in our parents' kitchens. No corn syrup? Hey, no problem—just use corn oil. No flour? Just use some ancient pancake mix instead. (Please don't try these at home.) Ironically, this substitution mentality eventually morphed into the way I develop recipes as a natural food chef today . . . only now, I "make something" with a healthier outlook, a more experienced and educated starting point, and, thankfully, a much higher rate of success.

My early foodie beginnings led to an ambitious adolescence spent in the kitchen, making recipes, rather religiously, from cookbooks in my free time. Every recipe taught me something—and although I didn't know it in the beginning, my mistakes were just as important as my triumphs, since an important part of knowing "why" is understanding "why not." My cookbook library was essentially my culinary school; my friends and family the critics. I was the Energizer bunny of recipe making.

But years later, when I first discovered superfoods in college, I was suddenly forced to give pause. Most of these exciting yet unique health-giving ingredients, such as goji berries and spirulina, weren't in any of my cookbooks. Even in the case of more common superfoods, such as strawberries, recipes often seemed to defeat any healthful purpose (hello 2 cups of sugar and 1 cup of heavy cream). It was at this time that I went back to my roots, my way-back-when roots, and started (tentatively at first) utilizing substitution methods to transform some of my favorite snacks into superfood-infused treats that really lived up to their name of *super* food. For the first time, I made my *own* recipes. And, thanks to my accrued kitchen experience, this time nothing exploded.

Right from the start, snacks were, and still are, some of my favorite things to make with superfoods . . . for a few reasons. First of all, I am, without a doubt, what most people call a "grazer"—I eat frequent mini meals throughout the day, which keeps me feeling my best, energetically speaking. But second, after experiencing the feel-good benefits of a superfood-infused lifestyle, I became very opportunistic with the way that I look at food. I feel that if you're going to make something craveworthy, why

not sneak in some healthy things at the same time? Why not have a few benefits mixed in with your favorite crunchies and munchies? If you could satisfy your sweet craving and get, for example, 10 grams of protein, a quarter of the fiber you need every day, and heart-healthy antioxidants as well, I mean . . . *why not*? Eating healthfully doesn't have to be limited to a lunchtime salad, nor does a "healthy snack" equal a plate of celery sticks. I believe it's not just about rethinking *what* we eat, but *how* we go about making what we eat. This impactful transformation is largely about the inclusion of superfoods.

Superfoods give us a new lease on treating ourselves. Life is too short to always "diet" and "deny." Instead, I think it's all about being smart with the ingredients we choose to use in the first place. So, the recipes in this book give you the freedom to celebrate every day with delicious snacks that are truly guilt-free, energizing, revitalizing, and even easy. Here you'll find traditional, naughty favorites that have been transformed into unique modern treats that are packed with powerful nutrition, while creating new tastes and pairing new flavors.

I am still impassioned about experimenting in the kitchen. But there's a difference now. With a nod to the exciting, if impetuous kitchen adventures of my adolescence, I've put in the time, since then, to carefully develop the recipes in this collection, so that the healthy (and delicious) triumphs can be all yours. So, my friend, it looks like it's your turn now.

Let's make something!
Julie

PART ONE

THE SUPERFOOD TREATMENT

Sure, the idea of "healthy indulgence" may first appear to be one of the most notorious oxymorons of culinary speak (much like "jumbo shrimp"); but, in fact, there's a whole world of smart secrets begging to be explored. It's not about denying our cravings; it's about discovering new, better ways to enjoy them. The secret, of course, is superfoods, which are at the epicenter of an exciting health revolution.

SNACKS: A HEALTHY WAY TO SATISFY

"Just listen to your body." I can't tell you how many people have given me this advice since I first started out on my health path at 20 years old. Yet, to be honest, for the longest time, I had little idea of what, exactly, that meant. Of course I tried to "listen." At first, I was pretty certain I heard my body suggesting that a large coffee and a frosted Danish was an inspired idea. But it didn't take long before I started to notice that my body was saying a lot of other things too (besides questionable menu requests): "I'm tired." "My head hurts." "I'm bloated." In fact, the more I listened, the more biological chatter I heard. And for the most part, it wasn't a particularly positive conversation.

In the midst of trying to resolve my personal health issues, a naturopathic doctor suggested I keep a food journal. I was assigned to write down everything I ate during the day, as well as how I was feeling before and after meals. Though it may seem obvious now, at the time the results truly surprised me: almost everything I was physically feeling throughout the day was *directly* linked to what I was eating. After my berry smoothie, I felt energized to go for a run. After I attacked a bag of peanut butter pretzels, I wanted to take a nap. My body wasn't giving me random signals. It was simply responding to my choices! It was then that I began to fully grasp how much control we really can have over how we feel.

Responding to your biological needs as they occur throughout the day, whether it's with a fresh snack, a healthy sweet treat, or just a little munchie,

is perhaps the most rewarding way of eating there is—and one that can satisfy the requirements of good health without compromising the flavors and textures you crave. But first, we have to re-learn how to speak the same language as our bodies.

HONORING OUR CRAVINGS

From pizza to potato chips to margarita-flavored jelly beans . . . why do these not-so-healthy food cravings occur in the first place? Certainly our ancient ancestors weren't running around collecting berries while secretly thinking, "Ugh, I would do a n y t h i n g for a chocolate croissant right now." They were probably thinking they wanted—craved even—the berries. That's because every craving means something very important at its core: it's a request from your body. Our bodies aren't here to sabotage our healthy efforts—in fact, it's just the opposite! They're designed to be receptive, intuitive, and intelligent when it comes to our biological needs.

Recalibrating the way that we listen and respond to our body's requests is the key to more rewarding eating and longer-lasting satisfaction. When you learn to eat instinctively, it's like drinking a tall glass of water when you're thirsty: It's the "ah, I needed that" moment. And you continue to feel better afterward, too.

Our cravings and food preferences are actually hard-wired into our brain and genes, stemming from our earliest days of basic survival, which is why almost everyone experiences them. Every nutrient has a direct effect on the body, on energy, and on mood. Carbohydrates aren't bad; they're needed to produce energy and stimulate the release of insulin—which ultimately increases serotonin, the neurotransmitter that regulates sleep, keeps us calm, and improves mood. Good fats are wildly important for all kinds of cellular function and have also been linked to serotonin production and stress reduction. And protein does more than just build muscle; it also helps stabilize blood sugar and it keeps all of our systems in balance.

Eating snacks throughout the day means we can address the fluctuating needs of our bodies with gentle micro-adjustments, keeping our mind, our body, and our resulting energy levels on an even keel. The key is knowing how to interpret our body's requests. Once we understand where our food cravings are coming from, instead of reacting to them with unhealthy snap decisions, we can better *respond* to them with smart choices that are truly satisfying on every level.

COMMON FOOD CRAVINGS

What we think we crave	What our body actually craves	Sample of balancing superfoods
Salty	Minerals, especially calcium	Dark leafy greens such as kale, sea vegetables, sesame seeds, chia seeds, spirulina, chlorella, mulberries
Sugary/Starchy	Glucose, sodium, chromium, serotonin/dopamine	Mulberries, dates, bananas, dulse, garbanzo beans, soy beans, quinoa, broccoli, goji berries, maca
Creamy/Sweet	Chromium, magnesium, protein/amino acids, chromium, carbon, phosphorus, sulfur, serotonin/dopamine	All nuts and seeds, avocado, goldenberries, cacao, hemp seeds, sea vegetables, watercress, kale
Caffeine	Iron, serotonin	Maca, nori, goji berries, goldenberries, mulberries, pumpkin seeds, hemp seeds, cacao, leafy green vegetables, wheatgrass
Chocolate	Magnesium, vitamin B12 and B6, antioxidants, serotonin	Cacao (raw dark chocolate), maca, walnuts, chia seeds, pumpkin seeds, hemp seeds, sea vegetables, spirulina, chlorella, acai berries, maqui berries, blueberries

Remember, cravings in their real form are actually very important cues. The more we truly listen to and nourish them, the less strong and overwhelming they become. This sets us up for long-term success in creating a truly healthy *lifestyle*. Making snacks out of real foods and incredibly nutrient-dense ingredients means we can enjoy our cravings as much as we like, ditch the feelings of guilt, and start enjoying the pleasure of multifaceted satisfaction.

SUPERFOOD SNACK PRINCIPLES

Knowing what our cravings mean is the first step. But satisfying their underlying cause is not always so easy. Most snacks found on grocery-store shelves don't exactly enjoy the best nutritional reputation. The majority of "convenience" snack foods are, unfortunately, composed of processed flour, refined sugar, excess salt, detrimental fats, and lab-created food additives—all of which add up to the "empty calories" about which we've heard so much. The good news? Snacks don't need to be limited to this contemptible category! Healthy snacks can have all the instinctual appeal of their nutrient-void counterparts while delivering myriad health benefits—not to mention great flavor and satiety—from much higher-quality foods.

Making *your own* snacks is not only often less expensive than anything you can buy at the store, it also allows you to have complete control over the quality of ingredients you consume, ensuring that every calorie is a functional, nutritionally-packed

one. The recipes in this book take this DIY concept and push it to its fullest potential: moving treats way beyond a "not as bad for us" status and into an incredibly beneficial one.

Superfood snacks enable us to address our taste buds (via flavor, texture, and aroma) as well as the roots of our cravings (such as a need for vitamins, minerals, protein, and more) by utilizing a carefully curated selection of ingredients, chosen to create otherworldly tasting recipes. So whether you're looking for something to ease a rumbling stomach at work, seeking the perfect post-workout treat, rousing up a healthy munchie for a movie on the couch, or just yearning for a special treat, rest assured you'll find it here.

To help you understand what makes superfood snacks so special, following are the core principles used to develop the recipes in this book. Keep them in mind as you move on to create your own "world's-best" treats!

1. LEAN ON WHOLE FOODS WHENEVER POSSIBLE.

When you're looking to make a creative healthy snack, the first stop in the hierarchy of choice ingredients is always whole foods: fruits, vegetables, whole grains, seeds, nuts, etc. You might not always be able to make a snack or treat entirely out of whole foods, but it's good to have this ingredient priority in place as you add things like sugars or oils (only as needed) for flavor and texture. For example, whole foods such as avocados or almond butter can sometimes be used to replace vegetable oil; and fruit can be used in lieu of some of the sugar in a recipe. Choosing whole foods means you get the benefit of the entire natural food package—sweetness, fat, or flavor that's also mixed with fiber, protein, extra vitamins and minerals, and more. This simple choice will help you feel fuller, longer. And when your snacks are more satisfying and energizing, it will lessen the likelihood of overeating, too. Even if you do accidently overeat a whole-food snack, you'll find your hunger and cravings more effectively reduced long term (as opposed to eating a less-nutritious snack where the brain continues to send out signals of hunger until certain nutrient requirements are met). In short, the more whole foods, the better.

2. PRACTICE AN OPPORTUNISTIC APPROACH TO BEST-CHOICE INGREDIENTS.

Snacks are a wonderful medium to incorporate many of our healthiest foods and superfoods. Who doesn't get excited about having a treat? So when they're filled with good-for-you ingredients, practicing a healthy lifestyle quickly becomes a whole lot easier.

Superfood snacks utilize the same idea of nutrient density that defines individual superfoods. Each ingredient has a specific purpose in both form and function: Everything is used not only to add flavor, but often to act as a smart substitute. And there's a vast selection of better-choice ingredients from which to choose! Coconut oil instead of butter. Goji berries instead of raisins. Almonds instead of peanuts. Ask yourself, "How can I boost this recipe a little bit more?" Seize the opportunity to do something extra-great for yourself every time you eat.

Within this opportunistic approach, perfection is not as important as progress. In other words, if utilizing a little sweet, no-calorie stevia "spares" a recipe an extra 2 tablespoons of sugar, it's a welcome success . . . even if there's still some sugar in the recipe. Every effort, every healthy act, counts—it all adds up. As you read about the pantry items you'll need to set up your own superfood kitchen on page 6, look for opportunities to make smart, exciting, and delicious superfood substitutions in your *own* recipes—and turn up the nutrition just a little higher.

3. INCORPORATE SUPERFOODS.

As you may have suspected from the title of this book, adding superfoods to your snack mixtures is the not-so-secret key to elevating them to new heights of nutrition and healthy balance! Even more exciting, it's much easier than you may think to make all of this happen. Though some of the recipes in this book utilize creative tricks to sneak in an extra boost of superfood power, there are many simple ways to add superfoods to just about any kind of snack under the sun, every day. Because superfoods are so profoundly dense in nutrients, you don't need much of them (sometimes as little as a quarter teaspoon will do); and every tiny pinch genuinely does contribute to better health.

To fully grasp just how powerful superfood ingredients are, as well as how to use them, check out The Superfood Snack Pantry that follows. And if you're a fellow superfood overachiever, be sure to check out the Superfood Boosts that are scattered throughout the book that elevate the recipes to even more amazing heights.

4. VALUE THE YUM FACTOR.

No matter what anyone says about how good and healthy superfoods are, there's still one undeniable truth about snacks: If they don't taste good, you probably won't eat them. Never deny the power of delicious! Arguably, the most important ingredient in sticking with a healthy diet over the long term is enjoyment. The recipes in this book still use small amounts of ingredients, such as smart sweeteners, healthy fats, and sea salt, etc., to help balance taste and make your superfood snacks completely irresistible. I look at these ingredients as my "flavor motivators." If following a stricter diet works for you, then please, of course, continue on your journey. But as a flavor hound myself, I believe that if a teaspoon of oil per serving transforms a boring, superfood-packed cookie (and sometimes, it truly can) into a crazy-amazing one that you can't wait to gobble, then that oil serves a good purpose! Experiencing "yum" is a form of happiness, and happiness is an integral part of overall wellness— making a balanced amount of vitamin Y (Yum) as important as any other essential nutrient. Don't eat anything you don't truly love . . . and truly love everything you eat.

THE SUPERFOOD SNACK PANTRY

The world of superfoods is huge!—from everyday foods that are already in your refrigerator (such as spinach) to celebrated foods from all around the globe (such as maca powder). Superfoods are simply the most nutrient-dense, benefit-rich foods found in nature. Per calorie, these foods offer exceptionally high quantities of healthy goodness; and when you incorporate these special ingredients into recipes, they help you get the most goodness out of each and every bite you take. Superfoods are the perfect example of "not all calories are created equal," in the very best sense.

Eating superfoods leads to long-term satiation and satisfaction. Once you start eating them, you will begin to crave the superfood snacks in this book, as well as enjoy the energy, mental focus, physical performance, and wellness they offer. In other words, once you get into the superfood routine, you will not only get to eat what you crave, but with time, you'll genuinely crave better and better food choices.

SUPERFOOD BOOSTS

New superfoods are constantly being discovered— in fact, it's an extremely exciting, continually growing world of wellness! In my career as a chef who specializes in superfoods, I love working with these ingredients because they are part of a scientifically based health revolution.

In this section you'll find a carefully selected group of superfoods that are particularly excellent for snack making and have been chosen for the incredibly valuable benefits they offer, as well as for their availability. There are many, many more superfoods in the world, but in the interest of helping you to create a bit of a "base camp" superfood pantry, these are the ingredients that are featured in this book. Though some may seem obscure, initially, they are utilized in the recipes here again and again, so you'll find that you reach for them a lot while learning how to use them! Better still, many of these ingredients are shelf stable, so they'll last a long time. Remember, it wasn't long ago that no one in North America had ever heard of a chia seed (certainly not as an ingredient) . . . and now it is sold in bulk at major retailers such as Costco!

The way I see it, superfoods have stood the test of time and have been valued by various cultures for thousands and thousands of years. In reality, as "niche" as some superfoods may seem, they are really part of a widespread superfood renaissance—one that holds the keys to a significantly healthier society. Food knowledge is power, and in this case, it is also incredibly delicious.

Acai Berries

Pronounced ah-sigh-EE, this deep purple berry grows on tall palms in the Amazon and has a long-standing reputation as an energy and beauty food. Acai offers a deliciously addictive, creamy berry flavor with slight chocolate notes that enhance almost any recipe. It is an indulgent-feeling super-food that's difficult to refuse.

SOURCING SUPERFOODS

Most of the superfood ingredients called for in this book can be sourced at your local health food store. Alternately, you can easily order them online. Many options are listed in the Resources Guide on page 209.

Benefits Acai is a go-to "glow" food for several reasons. Its anti-aging vitamins and minerals are many—including calcium, phosphorus, beta carotene, and vitamin E. Low in sugar, acai is one of the few fruits that also offers healthy fats in addition to fruit-based carbohydrates in the form of essential fatty acids (EFA's) and monosaturated fats. These skin-friendly fats help slow down the release of fruit sugar into the bloodstream, which is one of the many reasons why the energy experienced from eating acai berries feels so steady and long term.

Acai berries also have a wonderful store of anthocyanins, the "beauty antioxidant" that encourages blood flow to all the organs of the body. Just for comparison, acai berries have almost six times the ORAC value (antioxidant measure) of one of the most popular and well-known North American superfoods—blueberries. Because the acai berry's nutrition also appears to encourage stem cell production according to new research, it's no wonder that acai is often considered a top-choice superfood for recovery and rejuvenation by athletes, health enthusiasts, and wellness professionals alike.

Varieties The best acai products are the ones without any added sugar (giving you, the consumer, more control over your total daily sugar consumption). This is why refrigerated, commercial acai berry juice blends are not recommended for use in this book, although they do taste delicious. For making snacks, **acai powder**, which is made from freeze-dried acai berries, is ideal as it allows you to be incredibly creative in its application. Though it's not the least expensive ingredient on the block, it's very concentrated so you'll only need a little to get the benefits (and you'll get many, many servings out of a single bag). Acai berry powder is also shelf stable, so it will last for several months. Note: Although refrigeration is not required, I like to keep acai berry powder in the freezer to protect its sensitive nutrients and extend its shelf life.

Snack Ideas Despite the fact that cooking with acai damages much of its nutrition, and should be used for that purpose sparingly, acai remains a surprisingly versatile superfood. It's creaminess lends itself beautifully to puddings, sweet dips, and frozen desserts; and in its powdered form acai is a great addition to energy bars and fudgy truffles and bites. Adding a little natural sweetness to acai brings out its berry flavor even more, as you'll discover in Acai-Mint Stuffed Dates on page 133.

Algae

I know. The mention of algae doesn't immediately whet the appetite. And the fact that it tastes a little like the sea and turns everything it's mixed with greenish-blue, may not inspire a ton of excitement, either. But with one quick glance at the nutritional evidence and proven medical benefits of this food group (which represents the very first plants to appear on the planet), you'll likely fast-track ways to sneak this powerhouse into your diet! It's a favorite secret weapon for anyone seeking more energy.

Edible algae holds some of the most potent health benefits of any food you can possibly eat. In fact, some varieties of algae, such as spirulina, encapsulate so much nutrition that the antioxidant micronutrients found in just 3 grams (about one teaspoon!) surpass that of five full servings of any earth-grown vegetable. From a health standpoint, algae is worth its weight in gold. And a little bit of this green gold goes a very long way.

Benefits If edible algae such as spirulina and chlorella were laboratory inventions, and not nature-made microorganisms, scientists would probably think they had just invented a miracle supplement. Composed of 60% protein, algae rank as one of the densest sources of cholesterol-free, complete protein of all foods. (By comparison, beef contains just 22% protein.)

Algae is extremely high in a broad variety of carotenoid antioxidants—especially beta carotene—which act as strong protective agents against degenerative disease and premature aging. Algae is rich in vitamins—almost all of the B's, including bioavailable B_{12}, which is essential for neurological health, and many minerals, in particular iron, magnesium, phosphorus, and potassium. In addition, edible algae offer exceptionally dense levels of alkalizing chlorophyll that enhance the immune system. They even provide essential fatty acids.

Studies abound that link the regular consumption of even small amounts of edible algae to helping aid remission of multiple sclerosis, liver disease, allergies, diabetes, tumors, and a reduction of brain degeneration associated with disease and aging. Something tells me we've really only glimpsed the tip of the iceberg when it comes to the immense, truly amazing power of this superfood.

Varieties We're certainly not talking about just any type of algae here. Specifically, there are three main varieties of algae that are most popular: **spirulina** (a blue-green algae), **chlorella** (a green algae), and simply "**blue-green algae**," (which is the name under which it is sold). Each of these algae has minor benefits over the others, but all are wonderful. I find spirulina to be the easiest to use in terms of palatability in snack recipes, but you can definitely get away with substituting it for chlorella or another form of edible algae in any recipe, if you want to keep just one kind on hand. The aforementioned varieties are sold in powdered form (the way it is used in this book), as well tablets (which you'll need to grind into a powder before you can use them in the recipes).

Snack Ideas If you're not crazy about the ocean-like flavor of spirulina or chlorella, you're in luck. Because such small quantities are called for to give recipes superfood status, it's quite easy to hide the flavor. My favorite way to hide these algae is in darker-colored recipes, or at least, in ones which are already green, so the bright blue-green color doesn't give the contents away or make the recipe look like it belongs on a kids' Halloween table. Mixed into spice mixtures for nuts and seeds, stirred into herbed dips, or tucked away in fudgy raw chocolates, eating the best "greens" on the planet was never so craveable. Note that a large amount of the nutrition in algae is destroyed through heat, so it's best to use these superfoods in uncooked or very-low-heat recipes.

Cacao

There are superfoods for the body and foods for the soul. Cacao masterfully covers both. Cacao is where all that is good and right in the world of chocolate begins—there isn't a chocolate recipe or product on the planet that doesn't originate with cacao beans. It's wonderful and exciting to be able to enjoy a food in its truly natural state, the same way ancient cultures once did, and reap so many healthy rewards at the same time. Cacao and its corresponding healthy chocolate creations are the secret to composing some of the most indulgent superfood snacks ever!

Benefits Cacao is a bit of an anomaly—a superfood that makes the guiltiest of culinary pleasures fully justified by health benefits. A fiber-rich seed, cacao is a wonderful source of many minerals such

as iron, zinc, and sulfur. It's also one of the highest sources of magnesium—a mineral that offers general pain relief, reduces muscle cramps, promotes cardiovascular health, strong bones and teeth, and can even improve the quality of your sleep.

Cacao powder (the most nutrient dense form of cacao), is one of the highest antioxidant foods on record, with an ORAC value (which measures antioxidants) over 100 times greater than broccoli! The antioxidants in cacao are largely in the form of flavonoids, which numerous studies have linked to increased heart heath and better blood flow. Furthermore, cacao offers a fascinating repertoire of amino acids and phytochemicals (naturally occurring plant-based chemicals) such as phenylethylamine, tryptophan, theobromine, and small amounts of caffeine (though a fraction of coffee) that excite and energize the body, mind, and mood. No wonder cacao has such a feel-good reputation.

Varieties Cacao can be acquired in several different forms, but perhaps the best varieties for snack making are **cacao powder**, **cacao nibs** (pure crushed-up cacao beans), and—if you are making truly raw chocolate—**cacao butter** (the extracted cream-colored fat of the cacao bean). Unsweetened cocoa powder, which is the roasted or further processed form of cacao powder, is less beneficial, especially in the antioxidant realm, but it still offers many benefits and can be used in place of cacao powder (in a 1:1 ratio) if desired.

Snack Ideas Anywhere that chocolate is called for, cacao will easily and deliciously answer. You can make the most nutrient-dense raw superfood chocolate on the planet made from pure cacao, and even top it with additional superfoods for an extra kick. Or you can mix cacao powder into energy bars, sweet dips, and candies. Cacao nibs, which taste like unsweetened chocolate espresso beans, are a wonderful crunchy addition to cookies and baked goods, or as a topping for creamy sweets.

Chia Seeds

Even my friends who are new to superfoods find it easy to hop on the chia train. This tiny brownish-tan seed, once a celebrated staple food in ancient Central American cultures, is fast becoming a modern-day favorite health food and energy booster. In addition, since chia has virtually no flavor of its own, a better question than "What snacks can chia be added to?" is "What snacks can't chia be added to?" You can sneak a little, health-boosting chia into almost anything.

Benefits Chia is a pocket Hercules when it comes to all the nutritious value tucked inside every little seed. It boasts complete protein, dietary fiber (24% of the Recommended Daily Allowance in just 2 tablespoons!), and is one of the best plant-based sources of omega-3's of all foods. It's also an incredible powerhouse of micronutrients with every serving offering the same amount of calcium as ½ cup of milk, twice the iron and magnesium of a cup of spinach, and potassium that matches about a third of a banana . . . not to mention valuable antioxidants, such as anti-inflammatory quercitin, metabolism-boosting chlorogenic acid, and caffeic acid. I mean, wow, right?!

Chia is often viewed as an energy food and a weight-balancing food, in part due to its massive nutrition, but also due to its significant concentration of mucilage, a natural substance that helps plants retain water. Chia contains so much mucilage that it expands quite dramatically by forming a jelly-like exterior around itself when it comes in contact with liquid—one seed absorbs up to eight to nine times its weight in water. This means that each chia seed feels a lot bigger in the stomach then it actually is, making you feel full and sustained for hours, at a low-calorie cost.

Varieties Use raw/untoasted **whole chia seeds** for the snack recipes in this book. Brown (regular) chia seeds or "white" chia seeds can be used, since there is virtually no difference in taste or health benefit between the two. Another wonderful form is **chia seed powder.** This is simply composed of ground chia seeds and is a great way to sneak chia into flours and doughs virtually unnoticed. You can also swap chia seed powder for flaxseed powder anywhere you see it, as they perform very similar functions. Note that since chia seeds don't have a hard shell, they do not need to be ground before using. The difference between whole versus powdered forms is more a matter of culinary use than anything else.

Snack Ideas The mucilage in chia means that chia can become a truly functional culinary tool, as both a binder and a thickener, when combined with moisture. As a binder, chia can be used to create superfood-enhanced muffins, energy bars, and baked goods. And as a thickener, chia creates an indulgently textured pudding base (see Chocolate Protein Chia Pudding on page 61) and can be used in spreads to thicken and enhance the texture

without loading up on excess calories. All functionality aside, you can use whole chia seeds pretty much anywhere, and enjoy them as a sprinkle here, a spoonful there; I think they win the easiest-to-use awesome superfood award.

Berries (North American)

Munching on indigenous berries is perhaps the most "original" and ancestral superfood snack of them all. A good choice too, as these native fruits couldn't be more chock-full of benefits! Although there are many fruits that bring a wonderful store of nutrition to the table, berries rise above the rest in terms of nutrient density. Happily, the berries mentioned in the following list are most commonly available fresh (and sometimes even grown locally) in the United States, Canada, and Mexico. (Other incredible superberries must be shipped trans-continentally, and therefore dried or milled, to preserve nutrition.) The great news is that not only are berries a real treat, but there isn't an edible berry around that doesn't qualify as a real superfood! They ALL have superfood benefits.

Benefits and Varieties By and large, berries are primarily vitamin and antioxidant powerhouses with a good sprinkling of minerals too; and, especially for a fruit, they provide nutrition at notably low calorie and sugar costs. Though there are countless varieties of these little gems, here are some of the most common berries ideal for snacks—each of which offers a unique advantage.

BLACKBERRIES, BOYSENBERRIES, RASP-BERRIES When in season, these members of the caneberry family can almost always be sourced locally, and offer vitamins A and C, along with many minerals such as calcium, magnesium, and iron—making them a good berry choice for bone and teeth health. Plentiful antioxidants provide cardiovascular support as well.

BLUEBERRIES Anthocyanin antioxidants abound in these blue sweet-n-sour beauties, which rank high on the ORAC scale of antioxidants and offer significant anti-inflammatory and healthy heart benefits. Micronutrients such as vitamin C and potassium also make blueberries an exceptionally replenishing choice for exercise enthusiasts. When possible, choose wild-crafted (foraged rather than farmed) blueberries, as they will usually offer higher levels of micronutrients.

CRANBERRIES These tart, very-low-sugar red berries are especially nutrient-dense, with every calorie offering a concentrated supply of fiber; high amounts of vitamins C and A; many of the B and E vitamins; and also an excellent collection of minerals, from calcium to manganese. Additionally, cranberries have many wonderfully healing phytonutrients such as anthocyanins, quercitin, chlorogenic acid, and even lutein—a valuable carotenoid antioxidant that promotes the health of the arteries and protects against age-related eye disorders. And of course, as you may know, cranberries are also a long-celebrated natural remedy for urinary tract infections. While it is difficult to make use of fresh cranberries in the world of snacks due to their extra-tart taste, we can enjoy them in their sun-dried form. Look for varieties that are fruit-juice sweetened as opposed to ones containing added sugar.

STRAWBERRIES Although strawberries may win the vote for the most popular American berry, they are far from common when it comes to beneficial properties! Enjoying just eight medium strawberries is the equivalent of consuming about 150% of the recommended dietary allowance (RDA) of vitamin C! Plus, with minerals such as manganese, plenty of fiber, and antioxidants such as anthocyanins and quercetin, strawberries are a wonderful superfood for anti-aging, skin health and healthy joints, as well as heart and brain function.

Snack Ideas Just about any sweet recipe will benefit from the addition of berries! You can use fresh or frozen berries in baked goods, blend them into frozen treats, and incorporate them into spreads and superfruit leathers. Dried berries are wonderful in trail mixes and energy bars (just make sure they're sweetened with apple juice and not with sugar, and haven't been processed with the allergenic preservative sulfur dioxide). If you can find them, freeze-dried berries are a very cool way to add loads of berry flavor (and nutrition) to snacks, with their light-as-air, crunchy quality (I love adding them to crispy rice treats). And, lest we should forget while in our pursuit of culinary creativity, a handful of fresh berries à la carte is ALWAYS an A+ superfood snack!

Camu Berries

A cranberry-like, reddish orange berry prized in South America, camu is only beginning to take the rest of the world by storm. Its puckery-sour flavor may fail to get immediate high marks on the "yum" scale, but the camu berry quickly earns a prime spot in a healthy pantry thanks to its incredible nutrient contribution.

Benefits As "nature's vitamin C pill," camu berry powder (the form in which this ingredient is most often found in North America) offers a whopping 1180% RDA (recommended daily allowance) of vitamin C per teaspoon, with hardly any sugar impact—the highest quantity of any known fruit or vegetable! In fact, you'd have to consume more than eight oranges at once to get a similar vitamin quantity as a single teaspoon of camu berry powder. This is exciting because vitamin C is an essential nutrient for a huge variety of essential body functions, including disease prevention; accelerating healing; easing inflammation; and collagen production (one of the reasons why it's always lauded for being a true "beauty" ingredient). Camu is also a host for several amino acids that promote tissue growth and recovery, and antioxidant protection. To sum up, the camu berry is designed to protect and to heal.

Varieties Although the camu berry is a cherished fresh fruit in its local habitat, most parts of the world have access to it only in a powdered form (which is actually preferable from a snack-making perspective, as it's easier to sneak into a recipe). For the recipes in this book, we use **camu berry powder,** which is available in most health food stores or easily found online (see the Resources Guide for information).

Snack Ideas Because vitamin C is a water-soluble vitamin that breaks down quickly when exposed to heat, camu berry powder should only be used in snack recipes that do not require cooking. You'll find this powder is a great addition to energy bars and raw desserts for a vitamin C boost, and can also be tucked into puddings and dips. Camu rarely effects flavor as it is efficacious in very small quantities, i.e., ¼ teaspoon.

Flaxseed

Does every super seed have a Napoleon complex or something? There's hardly a nutritionist around who doesn't recommend flaxseeds, also known as linseeds, as a surefire way to supercharge a diet. And with a tasty, slightly nutty flavor, inexpensive price tag, and versatile culinary profile, flaxseeds are an ideal ingredient for making best-ever snacks.

Benefits Flaxseed is widely hailed by health professionals for its high concentration of omega-3 fatty acids, which make up a whopping 48 to 64% of its total fat content! And studies suggest that this exceptionally beneficial superfood can reduce the risk of coronary heart disease, lower bad cholesterol, and decrease inflammation throughout the body. Oh, and from a vanity point of view, it doesn't hurt that these omega fats also promote smooth, glowing skin, and lustrous hair. Additionally, the high fiber and mucilage content of flaxseeds help stabilize insulin and blood sugar levels, reduce the appetite (i.e., they make snacks more filling), and can help with bowel regularity.

An important difference between flax and its honorary cousin, chia, is lignin content. Lignins are plant estrogens that help maintain bone health and protect the body against estrogen-driven cancers. That flax also boasts vitamins D and E, as well as a full array of minerals such as carotene and lecithin, which makes it a very-well-rounded superseed.

Note: Although you should grind flaxseeds to access the greatest nutritional benefits, all is not lost by using them whole. The body can still use their fiber and mucilage for healthy digestion.

Varieties There are two main types of **flaxseed**: golden and brown, which can be used interchangeably (they taste almost identical). Superfood snacks also benefit from the use of **ground flaxseed powder**, which you can either buy at the store or make at home by grinding the whole seeds in a spice mill. For the longest shelf life, store your flaxseed powder (and even your seeds) in the refrigerator or freezer to prevent the fats from oxidizing.

Snack Ideas Flaxseeds are similar to chia seeds in the ways they can be used. In some recipes, using whole flaxseed creates a nice crunchy texture and mildly nutty flavor in cookies or sprinkled on top of a dip. Ground flaxseed powder can be used as both a flour boost, a binder, or a thickener such as in things like muffins, energy bars, or puddings. You'll also find flaxseed is incredible when used as a great omega-rich and cholesterol-free egg replacement in baked goods.

Goji Berries

This lipstick-red Himalayan berry has had the superfood sticker applied to it pretty much since it was first celebrated as a longevity food in Chinese medicine thousands of years ago. When dried, a goji berry looks like a red raisin—and tastes like one too—with a little bit of a cranberry note. Thanks to palatability, and the detectable energy boost they deliver, goji berries are consistently one of the most popular choices for creating superfood snacks.

Benefits Few other natural foods (let alone synthesized products!) compare to the profound nutritional completeness that goji berries offer. These special berries boast all of the amino acids (forming a complete protein), dietary fiber, low-sugar carbohydrates, and antioxidant-packed fat from the tiny edible seeds on the inside of each fruit. Add to that more than 20 vitamins and minerals, which, ounce for ounce, include more beta carotene than carrots, more vitamin C than oranges, and more iron than steak. Goji berries are often the subject of medical research because of their plentiful antioxidants. like zeaxanthin and lutein, shown to help improve vision and protect against neurological degeneration and Alzheimer's. Other studies have linked the goji's orchestra of micronutrients to enhanced immune-system function and cardiovascular support. Plus, goji berries are one of the few foods to be considered an adaptogen, meaning they help our bodies manage and balance stress as well.

Varieties Unless you have a goji vine growing in your backyard (which, by the way, you can actually grow in some parts of North America), the best source of this superfood for snack-purposes is **dried goji berries.** Goji berry juice and goji berry powder are on the market as well, but are not used in any of the recipes in this book.

Snack Ideas Dried goji berries seem destined for snack creations! They can be used just like raisins as a way to add a little bit of sweet chew to trail mixes and granolas, cookies and bars, and other baked goods. Goji berries also pair extremely well with cacao, so you can enjoy two superfoods at once!

Goldenberries

Engagingly tart with a sweet citrus zing, there's nothing subtle about the provocative flavor of goldenberries. This globe-like berry looks like a miniature orange-yellow version of a tomatillo—a little round gem dramatically displayed inside of a delicate, paper-thin husk—and is a prized fruit all around the world. If you're thinking to yourself, "Hey, those goldenberries sound a lot like our local _____ berries . . . I wonder if they're the same?" the answer in all probability is yes. Goldenberries have dozens of different names worldwide, including ground cherry, Cape gooseberry, and Inca berry!

Benefits Goldenberries have a long-standing superfood reputation. Like some of the top superfood berries, goldenberries offer all of the major macronutrients—protein (even more than goji berries); small amounts of fat; and low-sugar carbohydrates. They also serve as an excellent source of micronutrients such as beta carotene, vitamin C, and many B vitamins, as well as phosphorus. However, goldenberries are best known for their wealth of bioflavonoid antioxidants. These special nutrients, which work hand in hand with vitamin C, play a huge role in making the goldenberry a powerful anti-inflammatory and immune-boosting food that also has antiviral, anticarcinogenic, and antihistamine properties. Goldenberries are ideal for allergy sufferers—I always stock up on them during the grassy spring season!

Varieties As mentioned above, goldenberries go by many names (the official botanical name is *Physalis peruviana*, if we're getting technical here). They are occasionally found fresh in stores and markets, and may be used in this form to ramp up frozen desserts and fruit snacks. More commonly, and usually more cost-effectively, they can be sourced as **dried goldenberries**, gently dried like raisins, a process that beautifully condenses their natural sweetness and flavor. The recipes in this book use goldenberries in this form.

Snack Ideas Since goldenberries are like golden raisins—only with a whole lot more of a flavor 'tude—we can use them in a similar manner. Goldenberries have a way of adding something special to anything they're applied to, from trail mixes and energy bars to fruit sauces and sweet treats.

Grasses, Sprouts, and Microgreens

It may sound like a health nut cliché to tout the benefits of these baby greens, but in fact, there's genuinely something to this long-lasting obsession. As absolutely wonderful as mature vegetables are to eat, they are many, many times more nutritionally wonderful in their youngster form. As you may have surmized, nutrient density is at work here once again, which is why grasses, sprouts, and microgreens—from fresh and crunchy to powdered and condensed—make the list of some of the finest superfoods.

Benefits The process of germination transforms the nutrition of a seed from great to incredible, and because the plant is still so small, each sprout or microgreen is jam-packed with nutrition. These low-calorie foods contain excellent sources of amino acids, vitamins—especially beauty-boosting and immune-supportive vitamins A, C, and E—and minerals such as calcium, folate, and iron. In addition, there's plenty of fiber, anti-cancer phytochemicals, and antioxidants such as chlorophyll, quercitin, and isoflavones, which help balance the body's pH, fight inflammation, and protect us from degenerative diseases.

Not surprisingly, the juice that is pressed from some types of grasses (a different type of "sprout"), such as wheatgrass, is regarded as one of nature's most health-giving foods. And we can use the powder made from this juice to easily create incredible superfood snacks. Wheatgrass powder has more than 70 vitamins and minerals in it, and has long been considered one of the top detoxifying foods.

Varieties There are tons of fresh sprout and microgreen varieties, and our bodies welcome them all! Some favorite snack varieties include **fresh sunflower sprouts, radish sprouts, clover sprouts, sweet pea greens**, and **microgreens** in varieties such as beet or arugula. There's really no wrong answer in this sprouted vegetable category.

As far as grasses go, the two most palatable are generally **wheatgrass powder** and **barley grass powder**. Both are interchangeable in a recipe, but I tend to lean toward wheatgrass powder because of its slightly sweeter taste. For best value and nutrition, seek out a freeze-dried wheatgrass powder that is made from 100% wheatgrass juice, not one that is composed of milled whole wheatgrass blades. The dried juice is a much finer, more nutritionally condensed product (a serving amounts to a miniscule ¼ teaspoon), that is gluten free and much more palatable than the milled product. You can find my favorite brand, which is used to develop and test the recipes in this book, in the Resources Guide on page 209.

Snack Ideas Admittedly, sprouts and grasses are not always the go-to ingredients for snack purposes, but with a little creativity, they can be incorporated successfully. First, it's motivating to remember that *anything* sprouted is an instant nutritional step up. If at the store you spot any kind of sprouted grain flours, sprouted nuts or seeds, sprouted legumes, etc., you can easily swap them in for their "regular" counterparts in recipes and get an instant nutritional gain.

Fresh vegetable sprouts and microgreens are more of an accouterment in the snack realm than anything else—but they're great to have on hand to sprinkle over a hummus-topped cracker or toss into a quick roll or wrap. In fact, they're one of those foods that can be added to virtually any savory food as a quick and easy boost. Wheatgrass (or barley grass) powder, on the other hand, is perhaps the easiest way to sneak sprouted nutrition into the broadest spectrum of snack foods. Thanks to a mild flavor that can easily be masked, and a high nutrient concentration (that makes it possible to use in small amounts), these green powders can be mixed into uncooked sweet treats such as raw cookies or truffles, incorporated into best-ever energy bars, or mixed into savory dips. (I like to use them in applications that are already green, so as to better disguise these greens and not give away the superfood "secret.") And once again, it bears repeating: Be sure to use sprouts only in recipes that do not require high heat, or else you'll cook away most of their vitamins, which are heat sensitive.

Hemp Seeds

With hemp seed's soft texture and lightly nutty flavor reminiscent of sunflower seeds, it's certainly not difficult to understand why any foodie worth his or her fork would happily get behind the infinite culinary uses of the tiny hemp seed, which is about the same size as a sesame seed. Though a rising novelty star in the kitchen, hemp seed is anything but new. Hemp was one of the first and most eco-friendly crops grown in the original U.S. colonies. In fact, hemp was one of the first plants ever cultivated, with a recorded history of over 12,000 years!

Benefits Hemp is a true superfood standout seed that provides all of the essential amino acids—a wonderful way to add plant-based protein to our diet via delicious recipes. Just 1½ tablespoons of hemp seed offers 5 grams of protein, and extra-condensed hemp protein powder can provide even more! Hemp seeds also rank as one of the best sources of balanced essential fatty acids—omega fats cannot be synthesized by the body and must be sourced through diet. These fats are imperative for cellular growth and tissue health. Hemp seeds are even a plentiful source of GLA (gamma linolenic acid), a specific type of omega-6 fatty acid, which reduces inflammation and has been known to help fight heart disease as well as high cholesterol.

Additionally, hemp offers dietary fiber, vitamin E, and minerals such as magnesium, iron, zinc, and potassium. Unlike some other nuts and seeds, hemp seeds are not a known food allergen.

Varieties The recipes in this book use hulled raw **hemp seeds**, which are sometimes called **hemp hearts**. (Toasted unhulled hemp seeds—usually salted—are also becoming increasingly available as a crunchy snack all on their own, but they are not used as an ingredient in *Superfood Snacks*.) **Hemp protein powder** is also called for in some of the protein-packed snack recipes. For best results, use a pure protein powder with the least amount of fiber (and therefore, the greatest amount of protein). For recommendations, take at look at the Resources Guide on page 209. If you like, as an alternative you can use your favorite protein powder blend that has hemp in it, but keep in mind that it may alter the flavor of the recipe.

Snack Ideas Small and soft, hemp seeds can easily become a favorite ingredient when creating superfood snacks . . . they're just so wholesomely delicious! Mix them into granolas, bake them into cookies, fold them into dips, or press them into homemade crackers. In fact, you can give almost any recipe in this book a superfood boost with the addition of a little hemp.

Leafy Vegetables

Not every superfood is an exotic underdog, and leafy greens are a perfect example of that—they are among the very best foods we can consume, so please do take every opportunity to crunch, chop, blend, and sneak these powerful green foods into your favorite treats and snacks.

Benefits Talk about benefits galore! With an extremely high (and broad spectrum) micronutrient content, at a very low calorie cost, leafy vegetables are some of the finest examples of nutrient density. Although every green offers a slightly different composition, this class of foods is exceptionally high in vitamins such as C and E and beta carotene, as well as folic acid, which is needed to build and protect DNA structure. (A crucial pregnancy and anti-cancer nutrient, folic acid is, unfortunately, one of the most common vitamin deficiencies.) Leafy greens also supply many minerals from bone-building calcium to blood-building iron. And they contain plenty of tumor-reducing fiber and more antioxidants than you can shake a stick at. Every year studies pour in on the important role of these superfoods, making it clear that incorporating a variety of leafy vegetables into your diet every day is one of the most rewarding healthy choices you can make.

Varieties Some of the best varieties of leafy greens for snack making include **kale, Brussels sprouts** (I promise!), **spinach, Swiss chard, collard greens, lettuce, broccoli, radicchio, endive, sprouts, microgreens,** and any fresh **green herb**—from **parsley** to **basil**—and **greens powder.** If one of your favorite greens is not on this list, I have two words for you: use it.

Snack Ideas Just because it's a vegetable doesn't mean you have to save it for a salad or side dish. There are plenty of ways to use leafy greens in craveworthy snacks. Dehydrating dark greens, such as kale or collards—or baking them at a low temperature—can create thoroughly addictive crispy "chips" that even kids can't stop eating. You can also sneak in extra nutrition by blending mild greens such as baby spinach into various batters for baked treats or into savory hummus-type dips. Pliable lettuce or collard leaves make great wraps for a delectable spread and a crunchy item or two, adding up to a smart and satisfying solution for a two-minute mini meal. And adding concentrated greens powder blends (see recommendations on page 16) into energy bars and even chocolate truffles is a wonderful way to make green foods irresistible to even the most finicky palate.

Maca

Do you really want to FEEL the difference that superfoods can make? Are you looking to increase energy, stamina, and strength (and who isn't)? Then look no further than maca, a Peruvian root with a bold malty flavor, which pairs beautifully with chocolate, nuts, sweets, and grains. Maca powder is also becoming a treasured staple in the superfood pantry and easily earns its keep as one of the most powerful foods in nature.

Benefits Maca root is famous for helping keep us energized and balanced, mainly due to the almost 60 phytonutrients it brings to the table. In addition to vitamins (including some of the energy-giving B vitamins), amino acids, fatty acids, and fiber, maca is particularly potent in minerals, offering close to

31 varieties, which it sucks up from the rich soils of the Andes highlands. These minerals include high amounts of potassium, calcium, and energizing phosphorus, which influences ATP (adenosine triphosphate) production, an essential component of intracellular energy transfer. Maca is also an excellent source of a variety of plant sterols—beneficial steroid-like compounds that can lower cholesterol levels and, according to recent studies, appear to prevent the onset of Alzheimer's disease.

What really sets maca apart from many other superfoods is its role as an adaptogen, a rare class of plants that restores and supports adrenal function and offers sustainable energy without being a stimulant (like caffeine). This property also helps regulate and reduce stress, resist disease, and regulate hormonal and biological balance. Maca is also a well-known natural libido booster and fertility enhancer. Only 1 in about 4,000 plants offers adaptogenic properties; and among these, maca is one of the few that can be used both as a food and a natural medicine. Needless to say, maca is a go-to superfood for making energy snacks that genuinely live up to their title.

Varieties Although maca is sometimes sold in tinctures or capsules, you'll want to use pure maca powder for snack making. There are two main varieties of maca powder on the market: **raw maca powder** and **gelatinized maca powder**. Raw maca powder usually contains just dried maca root that has been milled into a powder. It has the advantage of being minimally processed and contains more fiber. Gelatinized maca powder is a bit like a maca concentrate. The starch is removed from the maca before it is milled

into a powder, making it more concentrated in micronutrients, easier to digest, and slightly sweeter (there is no gelatin in this product, despite its name). Both raw and gelatinized maca can be used interchangeably for the snack recipes in this book. Personally, I veer toward the gelatinized variety because of its digestive advantage.

Snack Ideas Maca's flavor refuses to be hidden—instead it has to be celebrated or not used at all. While it usually doesn't work well with most savory or fruit-based snacks, its malty flavor plays nicely with a variety of sweets. Maca and chocolate are long-time energy and flavor buddies, and you can almost always add a little maca whenever you see cacao in a recipe. Maca works well in baked goods (just swap out a tablespoon of flour for a tablespoon of maca powder) and in rich puddings

and ice creams. It can also take on an almost butterscotch flavor when it pairs with other ingredients like nuts such as in the Butterscotch-Hemp Crispy Rice Treats on page 155.

Note: Maca is a very potent superfood. Bear in mind that "more" does not equate to "better." Most people find that one teaspoon to one tablespoon of maca a day is enough to sustain wonderful benefits, so the recipes in this book use just a small amount per serving.

Maqui Berries

In health circles, this vibrantly purple berry from southern Chile is often referred to as "the rainforest blueberry." While that's a pretty way of describing this gem of a superfood, I think of the maqui berry as a blueberry on steroids more than anything else! Maqui may not be strong in flavor (it offers just a hint of berry on the tongue), but whoa can it ever add a powerful punch in terms of nutrition!

Benefits To date, maqui is the #1 antioxidant fruit on the ORAC scale (Oxygen Radical Absorbance Capacity, the method used to measure antioxidants). Yes, maqui's score is even higher than acai, goji, and blueberries! With one look at this incredibly dense purple fruit, you can start getting some clues about where all those antioxidants are coming from. Maqui's primary antioxidant comes in the form of anthocyanin, a reddish/bluish/purplish hue. This antioxidant offers anti-aging benefits, enhances blood circulation (one of the reasons why it is considered a stamina-promoting food), and shows promise in reducing inflammation. Maqui also contains other nutrients, such as vitamin C, that are

wonderful for skin health, as well as trace amounts of minerals such as iron.

Varieties It's unlikely you'll find fresh maqui berries outside of a rainforest environment. Luckily, a powder is becoming more accessible. The powder encapsulates and preserves the nutrition of the maqui berry. Nutrients are activated when the powder is combined with food or moisture.

Snack Ideas When it comes to this superfood, the less heat the better. Enjoy maqui in no-cook recipes like puddings, energy bars, truffles, and frozen desserts, or use it in a seasoning mixture for an extra nutritional topping. Also, for more fun, watch maqui instantly turn light-colored snacks a vibrant, beautiful purple!

Mulberries

Anti-aging never tasted so good. Sweet mulberries—originally hailing from China and Turkey and now grown in many other areas around the world (including North America)—are purple or white and look like elongated blackberries. They offer a host of unique benefits. When sundried, they have a crunchy and chewy fig-like flavor with hints of vanilla that most people, from high-end chefs to little kids, find absolutely irresistible.

Benefits Mulberries may taste like sweet raisins but, in fact, they deliver all the same sweetness with less than half the sugar. Dried mulberries are high in digestion-friendly fiber (⅓ cup provides 20% of your daily needs), are good source of protein and calcium, and are rich in iron: with more than five times the iron of spinach. They are also an excellent source of vitamin C (a vitamin that, conveniently, increases iron absorption). Additionally, mulberries contain powerful antioxidants that help thwart free-radical damage, and are one of the few strong sources of resveratrol (the same anti-aging antioxidant that is found in red wine), which makes them especially good for heart protection.

Varieties There are two main types of mulberries: white and purple. If you have access to them, fresh mulberries can always be used in place of other fresh berries in recipes, but for the purpose of snack making, **dried white mulberries**, which are the sweetest, most flavorful, and most shelf-stable variety, are favored in this book.

Snack Ideas Mulberries can act as both a natural sweetener and a fiber-rich binder in recipes, making them enormously useful in almost any kind of sweet snack. They are wonderful when ground up into baked goods or cookies, used in raw treats, added to trail mixes, or blended into puddings. Sundried white mulberries are one of my favorite ingredients to use in snacks . . . as long as I don't eat all of them, by the handful, before I have an opportunity to use them in recipes!

Seaweed

Really, what is it about the salty, briny, savory goodness of seaweed that is so profoundly addictive, in the very best of ways? Could it be that our very cells respond with an instinctive, biological "YES! MORE!" whenever we taste the stuff, or is it just the craveable umami flavor that adds a delectable intrigue and makes our taste buds sing and dance? Either way, seaweed certainly isn't reserved for sushi chefs or used exclusively by health purists anymore, and any snack boosted with the power of sea veggies is instantaneously a smarter one.

Benefits There's a good reason why seaweed is a food staple in the diets of so many of the healthiest cultures around the world, such as East and Southeast Asia. The abundance of micronutrients found in sea vegetables far surpasses that of any earth-grown vegetable, thanks to the nutritious broth of seawater in which these plants flourish. Every seaweed brings its own team of benefits to the table, but most seaweeds (especially the dark-colored ones) offer a rich complement of vitamins, including B vitamins, which bolster the metabolism, and the oft-forgotten essential vitamin K, which is needed for blood clotting, liver function, and energy production. There are also impressive stores of antioxidants, essential amino acids, and essential fatty acids (including DHA, which is strongly connected to brain health) in seaweed. Seaweed is also known to offer antiviral, antibacterial, and antibiotic protection.

And then there's the exceptional mineralization, which is perhaps seaweed's biggest claim to superfood fame. These ocean vegetables offer a huge range of minerals but are especially rich in potassium, sodium, iodine, magnesium, and calcium—a perfect combination for those of us who lead an active lifestyle and need to replenish these elements frequently.

Varieties Hundreds of popular edible seaweeds are available now (see the Resources Guide on page 209), and each one comes with its own special profile, when it comes to flavor, texture, and culinary applications. For the purpose of simplicity, the recipes in this book use just three forms of seaweed: **nori sheets**, such as the ones used for making sushi (raw sheets are preferable, but an unsalted toasted variety is fine too); **dulse flakes**, which are the most versatile and easy to work with form of this salty red seaweed; and whitish translucent **agar flakes**, which offer almost no flavor at all but act as a gelling agent, making it easy and fun to use for textural creations. **Note:** Seaweed is only as good as the water it grows in and is susceptible to environmental toxins. Be diligent about always buying seaweed from clean waters—see my recommendation on page 209.

Snack Ideas So, you know all those great minerals we talked about? They're largely responsible for seaweed's salty flavor, making this superfood an excellent means to create salty snacks by adding something better than "just salt." Crispy nori, with just a touch of oil, salt, and sugar, has practically started a snack revolution all on its own (my friends' kids eat it like candy). Whole nori sheets make perfect low-calorie wraps for delectable dips and vegetable fillings, and hand-crushed nori sheets or dulse flakes can be sprinkled on popcorn, used in crackers, or whipped into spreads.

Super Grains

Cereal grains are a type of starchy seed that come from grasses. They're not only the most commonly used foods in the world today, but they also have been depended upon by humans for over 10,000 years! In their whole, unrefined form, grains can be a key component in a sustainable snack—a good source of slow-burning energy that provides a good balance of complex carbohydrates and protein. Yet some of these grains really go above and beyond the call of duty in the nutrition department, which is why we call them the best-of-the-best varieties of superfoods.

Benefits and Varieties Though there are many types of grains, the following are some of my favorites, and are used in several of the recipes in this book. With the exception of teff (which is a cereal grain), each of these is, in fact, considered a pseudocereal. Pseudocereals act like starchy ingredients from a culinary standpoint, but they do not come from grasses, as a true grain does.

AMARANTH This teeny-tiny yellow powerhouse is just slightly larger than a chia seed. Amaranth, native to the Americas, where it was once prized by the Aztecs, is a nice switch from the more popular superfood quinoa, and offers a similarly mild, slightly nutty flavor. With a 16% protein composition, it offers concentrated nutrition, including lysine—an essential amino acid that is important for the production of collagen and hormones. Studies show that lysine boosts the absorption of calcium, making amaranth a wonderful food pairing with another Aztec favorite: calcium-rich chia. Amaranth is also second only to quinoa when it comes to iron, plus it offers vitamin C, which is rare for a grain.

BUCKWHEAT It may have *wheat* in its name, but buckwheat is more closely related to rhubarb than any cereal, and is also gluten-free. A brownish tan seed that grows all over the world, including North America, buckwheat provides significant amounts of protein, and, like amaranth, it is also particularly rich in lysine. Buckwheat offers a slightly sweet, nutty flavor in the form of **buckwheat groats**, which are hulled, whole buckwheat seeds. **Buckwheat flour**, a dark brown flour made of finely milled groats, is a wonderful baking tool.

QUINOA A superfood kitchen favorite and "king" of the pseudocereal group (from the standpoint of

nutrient density), this small seed is native to South America and ranges in color from yellow to red to black, depending on the variety. (Remember that strong colors signal the presence of antioxidants, so while all quinoa seeds are good for you, the darker-colored varieties will give you an additional boost.) Quinoa is beloved because it "behaves" like a delicious, slightly nutty-tasting fluffy grain—without the gluten. It is also an excellent source of complete protein. In fact, a 1-cup serving of cooked whole quinoa offers 8 grams of protein (that's 25% *more* than an egg . . . without any of the cholesterol!). Quinoa is also a good source of lysine, calcium, iron, phosphorus, and even vitamin E and some B vitamins. In *Superfood Snacks*, we use **whole quinoa** (any color is great) and sometimes **quinoa flakes** (rolled and flattened quinoa seeds). Although not used in this book, quinoa flour is also a wonderful way to add additional protein to baked recipes.

TEFF Teff is the tiniest supergrain of them all! This poppy seed–sized reddish brown superfood originally hails from Ethiopia, and is valued for its balance of protein, fiber, iron, and calcium. Because of its minute size, cooked teff has the consistency of sticky porridge rather than a fluffy grain, and it confers a little nutty sweetness to whatever it is used in. Both **whole teff** and **teff flour** are fantastic to use!

Snack Ideas All these healthy supergrains—amaranth, buckwheat, quinoa, and teff—are wonderful, versatile additions to the world of snack making. In their whole form, they can be cooked (or at least soaked) and added to cookies or baked goods as textural ingredients (try the Cherry Quinoa Granola Clusters on page 42 and enjoy quinoa for the true seed that it is!). Supergrains can also be made into porridge, crackers, and crisps (as a way of replacing nutrient-void flours), cooked in water or broth, and added to wraps. Plus, all of these supergrains can be found as milled flours, too—a great way to supplement gluten-free and nutrient-dense baking.

SUPERFOOD HONORABLE MENTIONS

Although the following "honorable mentions" are all true superfoods, they are used sparingly, if at all, in the recipes in this book. But if you do get an opportunity to use them, go for it!

Pomegranate
Cherries
Sea Buckthorn Berries*
Noni*
Sacha Inchi Seeds*
Wheat Germ*
Medicinal Mushrooms*
Aloe*
Baobab*
Green Coffee Bean*
Cupacu*
Elderberry*
Kelp*
Mangosteen*
Lingonberry*
Matcha*
Phytoplankton*
Moringa*

*This ingredient is not used in any of the recipes in this book.

GOOD FATS

Fats—the good ones, such as essential fatty acids and monosaturated varieties—are a very important part of a well-rounded diet and have their place in healthy snacks, too! They make snacks more enjoyable, energizing, balanced, and satisfying over the long term. Used in moderate amounts, fats are an integral part of a primarily whole-food, plant-based diet. Plus, I don't know about you, but I'll take a little bit of good fat to create a treat that's over-the-moon amazing over a nonfat "sorta" good treat ANY day! Heart-healthy olive oil, skin-enhancing avocado, and high-heat friendly safflower and grapeseed oil are just the beginning. Get to know some of the advantageous fats that you'll find in many of the recipes for *Superfood Snacks*.

NUTS AND SEEDS

Talk about a primal food choice—nuts and seeds have been a staple energy source for humans in every culture since . . . well . . . since the beginning of humans! Our instinct to eat these foods is positively justified: Both raw nuts and seeds are tiny embryos—little capsules that contain a highly nutritional "recipe" to make a baby plant.

Nuts and seeds are an ideal choice in the realm of fats because the fat they offer is imbued with so many other benefits. Plant embryos contain everything needed to sustain the beginning of life: fiber, concentrated protein, healthy fats, vitamins, and minerals. In other words, nuts and seeds are among the most nutritionally charged foods that are available to us. Although nuts and seeds have long been touted as an important part of a healthy diet, a 30-year Harvard study recently confirmed the beneficial relationship of nuts to longevity. People who eat nuts every day reduce the risk of dying from heart disease by 29% and from cancer by 11%, and they tend to be slim.

The world of edible nuts and seeds is a vast one and, although some are more nutritionally dense than others, each seed and nut has its benefits. For example, pepitas (hulled pumpkin seeds), are a very high source of magnesium; walnuts offer an exceptional

amount of omega-3 fatty acids; Brazil nuts are one of the very best selenium-rich foods; and hemp seeds are especially high in protein and skin-boosting vitamin E. The list of nutritional benefits offered by this group of superfoods goes on and on.

When it comes to using nuts and seeds as ingredients in recipes, their protein and fat make recipes decadent and filling. Plus, their flavor profile is so versatile, it can easily meld with fruit in sweet desserts as well as with vegetables and other forms of savory protein. (Of course, the love affair of seeds and nuts with chocolate is legendary.) They can be used whole or chopped, and you can enjoy them as a satisfyingly crunchy element in almost anything you eat. Nuts and seeds can also be blended into a rich, dairy-like cream or processed into luxurious butters. And of course you can enjoy them as delicious, energy-sustaining snacks just by themselves,.

Since every variety of nut and seed offers its own unique flavor and texture, rotating your choices keeps snacks interesting and constantly new. Some of the nuts and seeds you'll find in the recipes in this book (in addition to the "super seeds" mentioned in the Superfood Boosts section on page 6) include coconut, cashews, almonds, walnuts, pecans, Brazil nuts, pistachios, pepitas, sunflower seeds, and sesame seeds.

NUT AND SEED BUTTERS

Good nut and seed butters—the thick, indulgent pastes that are made exclusively from nuts and seeds—can work just as well as conventional oils in some recipes, while adding extra nutrition. You can buy good nut and seed butters at the store, it's true,

but the ones you make at home will taste fresher and cost less than store-bought butters (explore the recipes for various superfood butters on pages 113–116).

COCONUT BUTTER

Just as you might expect almond butter to be a little different from almond oil, you'll find that coconut butter is not the same as coconut oil, despite their similar white, pasty appearance inside the jar. While coconut oil is a pressed oil and nothing more, coconut butter is made from the entire flesh of the coconut, so you get plenty of healthy fiber along with the oil. Believe it or not, the inclusion of coconut meat in the butter makes a huge difference in flavor (it tastes much more coconutty than the oil), and contributes a lovely creaminess to the texture. And although coconut butter may seem like a delicacy, in terms of ingredients it is transformational in creating delicious snacks —especially raw sweet treats that require a certain amount of solidity—by providing a melt-in-your-mouth experience. Coconut butter is increasingly found in natural food stores. (To learn how to make your own coconut butter, see page 114.)

Note: Do not substitute coconut oil for coconut butter, or vise versa—they perform quite differently in recipes.

COCONUT OIL

As far as oils go, coconut oil is really an all-purpose go-to, and I think it belongs in every pantry (including my grandma's kitchen, where, I'm proud to say, it holds a place of honor!). With its slightly buttery flavor, coconut oil makes a wonderful butter substitute in both sweet and savory recipes. Although it is, primarily, a saturated fat, coconut oil originates from a plant and does not cause a rise in bad cholesterol (LDL). It is also antibacterial and antiviral.

Coconut oil is considered a very stable fat for cooking, with a low risk of oxidation. There is little nutritional difference between refined and unrefined varieties, but refined coconut oil will offer a more neutral flavor. It will remain white and solid until it is heated above 76°F, when it will soften and eventually turn into a clear liquid (melted coconut oil, as it is referred to in the recipes in this book). As the oil cools, it returns to its solid state without losing any nutritional value. Coconut oil does not need to be refrigerated, and should be stored at room temperature so that it stays soft and easy to use.

HEMP OIL/EFA OIL

With its mild, nutty flavor, hemp oil is a wonderful addition to recipes that don't require high heat, and it is ideal as a finishing oil to drizzle over just about any food you love. Unlike most other oils, hemp oil is very rich in concentrated essential fatty acids (EFAs) that contain omega-6s and omega-3s in what some people consider to be in perfect balance to support optimum health. These fatty acids, which cannot be made by the body and must be obtained through diet, are strongly linked to optimized brain function and improved immunity, as well as beautifully soft skin and shiny hair.

There are several other oils that offer both strong EFA levels and a mild nutty flavor, which make them ideal for snack making. These include flaxseed oil, sacha inchi oil, and even specialized

EFA oil blends. Whichever you choose, make sure to keep these oils refrigerated after opening them, as their sensitive fats are best preserved in cold temperatures and away from sunlight.

SMART SWEETENERS

The pleasure we derive from eating sweet foods is purely instinctual and visceral, and one that must surely have been originally intended to signal the body that a high-calorie, quick-energy food was just the ticket. Of course, it's been a long time since we've needed any sort of signaling to prompt us to eat sweets for anything so basic as pure survival. Nevertheless, sweets are still one of the most pervasive cravings, and though they are not always rich in benefits as individual ingredients, sweeteners do have their place in making foods taste irresistible . . . or in our case, making healthy foods taste irresistible! The good news is not all sugars are created equal, so in *Superfood Snacks*, we rely upon a collection of "smart sweeteners"—or, sugars with benefits. Inspiringly, there's a growing collection of these smart sweeteners to chose from in the marketplace, but for simplicity's sake, the recipes in this book highlight only a small collection of go-to items.

FRUIT

Fresh fruit, dried fruit, pureed fruit, and fruit juice are all first-choice ingredients for sweetening snack and treat recipes, and are the only bona fide "beneficial" sweetener around. Fruit is most ideal because every sweet calorie is packaged with additional micronutrients and fiber to help create quicker satiation and enhance wellness. Some of the fruits that are used as sweeteners in this book's recipes include fresh dates, bananas, raisins, applesauce, apple juice, and grape juice.

STEVIA

Made from the leaves of a South American herb (which now grows worldwide), stevia is a remarkable natural sugar substitute. Stevia contains no calories, no sugars, no carbohydrates, and is 0 on the glycemic index, despite the fact that it is 3,000 times sweeter than table sugar! Although it is truly a "free" sweet ride, stevia does not work in every type of recipe, and it's easy to use too much, which can result in a sharp, flat, and occasionally bitter taste. Stevia often requires another kind of sweetness to balance it out a bit. Nevertheless, stevia can be used to reduce the calories and sugars in many types of recipes, especially creamy or liquid treats. I recommend buying stevia in its liquid form: it is usually sold as a tincture, along with a little dropper, for easy measuring.

LUCUMA POWDER

A cherished South American fruit, lucuma is most famous for its sweet flavor profile, impressively low sugar content (and low glycemic index), and naturally occurring micronutrients such as beta carotene, niacin, and iron. Lucuma's delicious, maple-like flavor has made it an increasingly popular ingredient, and it is often used in ice cream.

HOW TO CHOOSE DRIED FRUIT WISELY

Having a wide variety of dried fruits on hand is a great way to satisfy sweet cravings while making your snacks continually interesting and exciting. When you are buying dried fruit, however, it's very important to read the ingredients on the package. Dried fruit should really consist of only one ingredient: fruit. But since that's not always the case, here's a few tips for choosing the best dried fruit for your recipes.

- **Watch for added sugar.** Dried fruit is sometimes sweetened even further with extra sugar—a great example of "hidden sugars," and exactly the type of thing we are trying to avoid by making our own superfood snacks. If sugar-sweetened dried fruit is the only kind that is available in your local stores, consider ordering a non-sweetened brand online, even in bulk if you desire, for a more economical purchase. Dried fruits last a very long time—and avoiding all that unnecessary sugar will help *you* last a long time too.

- **Choose fruit sweeteners.** In a couple cases of naturally tart fruits, like cranberries, you have to add *something* to make the dried fruit edible, so what can we do? Luckily, some manufactures spare us the cane sugar and use apple or grape juice instead to sweeten. Brilliant! This is a great "natural" way to heighten the flavor of the fruit, without adding more sugar than you need. Look for these at the store, or order them as needed.

- **Check the preservatives.** Not all preservatives are bad. Ascorbic acid, for example, is simply vitamin C, and extends the shelf life of the fruit. Unfortunately, dried fruit is often pumped full of some other not-so-nice preservatives—namely sulfur dioxide— to make the packaged items softer. Sulfur dioxide is not easily digested, compromises the immune system, and is often the culprit behind allergies. Any time I pick up a product at the store and see sulfur dioxide on the package, it immediately goes right back on the shelf.

Since lucuma is not readily available fresh in North Amercia, it's convenient to purchase it in its powdered form, which is made from 100% fruit. Chock full of goodness, a little lucuma powder can be blended into a pudding, ice cream, or pastry flour to enhance sweetness at a low-sugar cost. It is best used in conjunction with another sweetener.

COCONUT SUGAR

Golden-colored coconut sugar is derived from sugar-giving Asian palm trees and has the distinction of being named the "most sustainable sweetener in the world" by the World Health Organization. It does not taste like coconut, as its name would imply, but it does have a slightly more complex sweet flavor that mimics caramelized sugar. As far as crystallized sugars go, coconut sugar is an ideal choice: at a glycemic index (GI) of 35, it has virtually half the glycemic index of cane sugar (which is usually around 68 on the GI). Coconut sugar also offers trace amounts of micronutrients such as potassium, zinc, magnesium, and several of the B vitamins. Best of all, coconut sugar is easy to use: It's a simple one-to-one replacement for cane sugar, and a go-to choice for many recipes.

AGAVE

This syrup extracted from a cactus is highly sweet, mild in flavor, and boasts a very low glycemic index (around 30), making it a popular choice for diabetics or anyone who is watching his or her blood sugar levels. Agave is certainly not without controversy, however, namely because its high natural concentration of fructose, which, while desirable for some people, causes concern for others. This is because fructose is metabolized differently from other sugars and transported to the liver, which can cause imbalances if consumed in high quantities. On occasion, I use agave because it boosts sweetness very efficiently, even with just a small quantity; but I am mindful about using it—usually as a way to boost another type of sugar. Agave is not a sugar to pour on with a "free ride" mentality like stevia. If anything, it falls into a gray nutritional area—I think agave is not "health-enhancing" per say, but rather is helpful when used moderately and in conjunction with other nutrient-dense foods.

MAPLE SYRUP AND SUGAR

Maple syrup and maple sugar are among the oldest sweeteners in North America. Both are made from the collected sap of maple trees, which is first concentrated through a process like reverse osmosis to develop a syrup. It is then boiled to intensify flavor and sweetness—and a higher sugar (primarily sucrose) concentration. The syrup is simply refined and sold as a liquid. To make maple sugar, the syrup is heated further to become concentrated and crystallized.

True maple syrup and maple sugar can be expensive, but their unique caramel and vanilla flavors add a welcome dynamic to many sweet and even savory recipes. The rich flavor of maple syrup also means less reliance on sweetness as a flavor element, so less syrup/sugar is required overall to keep it balanced in a recipe. Both maple syrup and sugar also contain small amounts of trace minerals, such as calcium and iron. Choose the darkest varieties available (such as "Grade B") to maximize flavor and nutrition.

YACON SYRUP

In its syrup form, you'd swear the delicious drizzle of yacon was some kind of artisanal caramel. But although yacon has all of the flavor appeal of a high-end sweet ingredient, in reality, it's simply a humble yet versatile root that looks like a potato . . . and one that has been cherished by Peruvians for thousands of years. Yacon's popularity is not solely due to its flavor, however; its health benefits are what make it really shine. Yacon is often used in Peru for blood sugar–sensitive diets, and provides sweetness in a recipe at a very low sugar cost. In addition to its low glycemic index, yacon's sugars are primarily composed of an FOS, short for fructooligiosaccharides. FOS is a type of low-calorie, nondigestible carbohydrate that tastes like sugar on the tongue, but is not processed as sugar by the body . . . and it even offers health benefits, such as promoting a balance of healthy bacteria in the digestive tract (i.e., it improves digestion). Add trace minerals such as phosphorus and potassium, as well as 20 amino acids, and you're left with an extremely beneficial ingredient as far as sweeteners go.

The only drawback to yacon is price. For this reason it is used only in very small quantities (and rarely, at that) in the superfood snack recipes in this book, and it can easily be replaced by any other liquid sweeter. If you decide to stash a bottle in your kitchen for special recipes, there is no question that you too will find yacon a sweetener to cherish.

THE POWER OF FLAVOR

Did you know that aside from transforming good snacks into thoroughly enchanting ones, almost every single edible herb and spice offers its own collection of superfood-like benefits, too? It's excitingly true: some of the most beneficial foods on the planet are already lurking in your spice rack and window box herb garden. Although, for the most part, herbs and spices can't be used in the same quantity as other types of ingredients in snack recipes, they can go a very long way, not only to boost flavor, but to enhance their health benefits, too.

HEALTH BENEFITS OF COMMON HERBS AND SPICES

Spice	Health Benefits
Allspice	Anti-viral, anti-bacterial, helps fight prostate cancer
Basil	Anti-aging, anti-inflammatory, reduces swelling and eases arthritis pain, helps treat irritable bowel syndrome
Black Pepper	Aids digestion, increases metabolism, may treat skin disorders such as vitiligo, helps prevent the spread of cancer
Cardamom	Digestive aid, natural energy stimulant, promotes heart health
Cayenne Pepper	Reduces inflammation, helps ease arthritis pain, boosts metabolism
Chili Powder	Regulates blood pressure, reduces pain, especially after surgery or therapy
Cinnamon	Helps control blood sugar, reduces bad cholesterol
Clove	Protects against heart disease, eases toothache, natural antioxidant
Fennel Seed	Aids digestion, helps prevent cancer and neurological diseases, natural antioxidant
Ginger	Aids digestion and fights nausea, soothes upset stomach, anti-inflammatory, reduces arthritis pain and swelling
Garlic	Protects against heart disease, protects against stomach and colorectal cancer, anti-bacterial and anti-viral
Mint	Soothes headaches, offers relief for common cold and sore throat, reduces symptoms of irritable bowel syndrome
Mustard Seed	Slows growth of cancer cells (specifically inhibits bladder cancer growth), improves circulation
Nutmeg	Anti-bacterial, boosts memory retention, boosts immune system
Oregano	Anti-bacterial, anti-fungal, reduces inflammation, boosts immune system
Parsley	Helps fight breast cancer, calms the nerves and adrenal glands, natural antioxidant
Rosemary	Improves digestion, enhances memory and concentration, reduces the formation of cancer

Sage	Antibacterial, anti-viral, aids digestion, natural energy stimulant, reduces inflammation, improves memory and mental processing, lowers cholesterol and triglyceride levels, natural antioxidant
Sea Salt	Tastes pretty similar to table salt—yeah, you guessed it: salty—but sea salt offers trace amounts of minerals, along with its flavor boost. And although sea salt crystals are larger than those of regular table salt they are, in fact, slightly lower in sodium: on average, 1 teaspoon of table salt contains 2,325 mg of sodium, whereas 1 teaspoon of sea salt contains about 1,872 mg.
Thyme	Reduces inflammation, treats acne, controls high blood pressure, protects against colon and breast cancers
Turmeric	Regulates hormones, boosts metabolism and regulates fat cells, improves organ functioning, anti-inflammatory, offers cancer prevention
Vanilla	Calms stomach pain, boosts mental performance
Wasabi	Protects against cancers, especially stomach cancer, fights obesity

SNACK-MAKING EQUIPMENT

When it comes to making the healthiest snacks around, the equipment listed here, from the obvious to the niche, are the true "tricks of the trade."

FOOD PROCESSOR

Food processors create miracles. One of the most jack-of-all-trades machines you'll encounter in the kitchen, a food processor is quick to handle all kinds of creative out-of-the-box recipes—from transforming beans and vegetables into an almost instantaneous delicious puree for dipping, to chopping up whole foods extra finely to help turn an otherwise "empty" dough into a virtuous one stealthily packed with superfoods. Truly, a food processor will be the dependable workhorse behind some of the most improbable yet successful snack concoctions you'll create.

BLENDER

A blender is as important to a superfood kitchen as a good knife. Unlike a food processor which chops and grinds ingredients, blenders truly blend, creating thinner types of liquids like drinks, creamy sauces, and extra-smooth puddings. Although there is no need to run and purchase a top-of-the-line blender for the recipes in this book (any blender will do the job), acquiring a high-speed blender is an excellent tool to have in your kitchen arsenal.

SILICONE SPATULA

This flexible, heat-resistant type of spatula makes it incredibly easy to get all kinds of mixtures out of bowls and kitchen appliances. You don't have to lose valuable ingredients just because a spoon doesn't reach or can't scrape the bottom of your blender. A silicone spatula acts as a manual windshield wiper to get all the good stuff off of flat surfaces as well as out of the curves in your kitchen machines. I like to keep at least two sizes handy: a small/medium spatula and a mini one for those especially hard-to-reach spots in the blender.

SILICONE MAT

Silicone mats are a godsend in the world of healthy baking. Instead of having to grease a baking pan with extra oil or line it with single-use parchment paper, silicone mats provide all of the nonstick benefits you need without any of the waste (or extra oil). The investment in these reusable, easy-to-clean mats is relatively small (with proper care they will last thousands of times) and their effectiveness is impressive. Are they a kitchen necessity? Probably not, and you can choose to stick with stand-by parchment in the recipes. But put a big star next to this environmentally friendly, budget-wise, and health-savvy product. (Note: A half-size mat fits perfectly on a standard baking sheet/cookie pan.)

CHEESECLOTH

A bit of this all-purpose cloth is always a smart thing to have on hand. Cheesecloth is better than a traditional strainer because it can be used to strain and separate liquids from solids with more control. And, as its name suggests, it's essential for making varieties of nut- and seed-based "cheeses."

DEHYDRATOR

You definitely won't need a dehydrator for any of the recipes in this book, but there are several snacks that can benefit from using this appliance, should you have one on hand (dehydrator-appropriate recipes will refer to this option in the instructions). Dehydrators have the unique ability to "cook" food simply with the flow of warm air—a process that mimics sun drying (most machines do not surpass 170°F). There are three main advantages to using this method: (1) More vitamins are retained in food, because they are never exposed to high heat; (2) there's no risk of overcooking or burning food, thanks to the extra-low heat setting (you can leave a dehydrator on overnight without worry); and (3) many foods are cooked more evenly because of the lower/slower cooking process. Just like a slow cooker, this slow "bake" takes much, much longer to create a finished product (sometimes a full day). This lengthy process may not make the dehydrator the first choice of busy cooks who need to produce food quickly, but the results are unsurpassed. Most people who use a range of kitchen appliances will attest that foods such as vegetable or kale crisps, seed-based crackers, and fruit leathers are best made in a dehydrator rather than an oven. Either way, a dehydrator is certainly a wonderful extra-credit item to have in the kitchen, especially if you feel motivated to create innovative nutrient-dense snacks on a regular basis.

REDUCING INGREDIENT COSTS

When you make your own snacks with superfoods, you're not only getting all the health benefits, you're also reducing costs by going the homemade route—we sure pay a premium for some single-serve, ready-made items! (I'm looking at you, $4 muffin). Even so, some superfood ingredients do come with an unfortunately hefty price; I tend to look at these ingredients as important investments (or cheap insurance). Do take comfort in knowing most dried superfood ingredients last for many, many recipes because the amount used in each serving is so small, which makes the per-serving cost actually much more affordable than it may initially appear. Additionally, as the popularity of superfoods continues to rise, the cost of some products is actually going down. I remember (very clearly) paying $40 for my first jar of goji berries over a decade ago. Now, I can purchase the same product for about a quarter of the price! But for the time-being, here are a few ways to keep your superfood kitchen as budget-conscious as possible:

Buy in bulk. Buying superfoods in bulk from bins or larger packages when available will cut down the per-ounce cost substantially. Before I became a professional recipe developer (and actually needed those large-size packages all to myself!) I'd often rope in a couple friends and we'd buy huge bags of things such as hemp seeds or goji berries by the pound or more, and then simply divided the ingredients amongst oursleves. The per-serving savings were huge.

Buy online. Although some stores do offer great deals from time to time, a little online hunting can often result in even better deals on superfoods, saving you several dollars at a time. Many sites offer free shipping, another convenient advantage to taking the online route. Sales change regularly, it's true, but getting a good deal is as simple as a Google search.

Buy in season. This tip is extremely important for limiting costs, especially when making recipes that call for fresh superfoods. If you choose to make a recipe with fresh blueberries in the dead of winter, you'll pay twice or even three times as much for them. Similarly, pomegranates in the summer will probably have a value similar to the gold standard. Instead, choose to make snack recipes that take advantage of seasonal produce, and don't be afraid to substitute when it's an option!

A superfood lifestyle doesn't have to be prohibitively expensive. Superfoods such as chia seeds, flaxseeds, leafy greens of all varieties, fresh berries, and "grains" such as quinoa and teff are relatively affordable options. Other superfood ingredients can be used one at a time or rotated, so there's no need to purchase every single one of them immediately, unless you want to! And remember, when you're looking to purchase nutrients and not just calories, superfoods are perhaps the best "deals" of all.

HEALTHY REWARDS OF SUPERFOOD SNACKS

I know, the sensation of a little something that just seems to hit the spot seems almost reward enough. But wonderfully, these recipes are designed ingredient by ingredient to serve a dual purpose, fusing the divide between totally delicious and truly healthy. Both the short term and long term wellness gains are expediential, but for some of the most core health benefits, look for these icons at the head of every recipe—an inspiring reminder of just how effectively you're really making the most out of every bite.

BEAUTY AND ANTI-AGING Snack contains ingredients that boast notable amounts of "beauty nutrients," such as vitamin C (essential for the synthesis of collagen and an anti-inflammatory agent), healthy fats like omega-3s, and various antioxidants for skin and cellular protection.

BONE STRENGTH Snack abounds in calcium-rich superfoods.

HEART HEALTH Snack contains superfoods with nutrients that have been shown in clinical trials to promote cardiovascular health.

IMMUNITY Snack is a good source of nutrients that fight disease, such as vitamin C and zinc, and/or contains superfoods renowned for having anti-viral, anti-bacterial, or anti-fungal properties.

LOW CALORIE Snack contains approximately 200 calories—or fewer!—per serving.

PROTEIN Snack has 6 grams or more of protein per serving.

PART TWO

THE RECIPES

....

From addictingly crunchy to luxuriously smooth, indulgently sweet to satisfyingly savory, let's face it: the idea of snacking really begs the question, "what do you feel like?" Excitingly, the incredibly vast spectrum of natural foods and superfoods offers the answer, on every level. Create simple grab-and-go Handfuls; grab a bowl and enjoy one of the many irresistible Spoonables; give packaged products a run for their money with best-ever homemade Bars & Bites; enjoy game-changing Crackers & Crips with power-packed Dips & Spreads; indulge smartly with Candies & Chocolates, or even Cookies & Pastries; enjoy any-time-of-the-day Frozen Treats; and get creative with extra-playful Kid Snacks. With a whole nourishing world of natural textures, color and flavor combinations at your fingertips, the world of superfood snacks is endlessly invigorating.

BEFORE YOU BEGIN

Incorporate these tips for cooking with natural foods, and the snacks that come out of your superfood kitchen will be stellar.

Test the consistency. You'll notice this phrase is used in many of the recipes in *Superfood Snacks*. Here's why: The amount of moisture varies in natural, whole ingredients, and this can have an effect on consistency and texture, especially if there is no cooking involved. To bypass this inconsistency of wetter versus dryer ingredients, don't be shy about making minor adjustments as needed to achieve an optimal texture.

Season to taste. While most recipes call for specific quantities of salt, pepper, and spices, you can always tailor them according to the flavor variances of fresh produce or just your personal taste!

Use liquid stevia. Stevia is an invaluable ingredient that helps boost the sweetness of recipes without adding additional sugar—don't skip this ingredient. When you are adding extra liquid stevia to a recipe, however, mix in only a drop or two at a time to raise the sweetness, as stevia is extremely strong.

Try these baking tips. To ensure accurate baking, always use the center rack of your oven. For best results, rotate the pan or tray (from front to back) halfway through the baking time.

Go gluten-free as needed. Almost all the recipes in this book are inherently gluten-free. Any recipes that are not gluten-free are clearly noted and include gluten-free ingredient substitutions,

DEHYDRATOR METHOD FOR SNACKS

If you have a dehydrator, it will really shine if you use it to make vegetable crisps and crackers. Dehydrators don't burn food, so you can dehydrate it at as low a temperature as you wish (for maximum nutritional content), or use a higher temperature for a faster cooking time. Simply spread wet food evenly atop 3 or 4 mesh dehydrator sheets, and dehydrate at the desired temperature until the recipe is crispy and dried through, usually after 6 to 12 hours.

all of which have been tested and work seamlessly. To find sources for gluten-free products, refer to the Resources Guide on page 209.

Substitute confidently. In some cases, substitutions, such as using a different type of dried fruit or another variety of seed, can easily be made. For a full breakdown of substitution suggestions, refer to the Superfood Substitution Cheat Sheet on page 207.

Source your ingredients. Most specialty ingredients are covered in depth in The Superfood Snack Pantry starting on page 6. You can find them at your local health food store or you can order them online (even at a discount sometimes). Stock up on a few of these superfood ingredients—they last for a long time—and you'll reach for the same ones over and over again as you become familiar with the recipes.

HANDFULS

Instinctually enjoyable, handful-type snacks are probably the most popular munchies in the world. From simple trail mix to power granola clusters, superfoods make many of these classic snacks come alive with flavor and nutrition. Featured superfoods include ancient pseudocereals like buckwheat and quinoa, dried berries, mighty seeds like flax and hemp, and even seaweeds to add minerals and salty flavor. There's lots to feel good about here, whether you're grabbing a swipe while out on the trail, or just curled up on the couch.

= FEATURED SUPERFOOD INGREDIENT

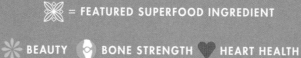

BEAUTY   BONE STRENGTH   HEART HEALTH

IMMUNITY   LOW CALORIE   PROTEIN

PROTEIN POWER TRAIL MIX

Making your own trail mix is pretty much the easiest thing ever, and you also get to control the quality of your ingredients from start to finish. Instead of using nuts, this well-balanced blend relies on seeds, edamame (whole soybeans), and protein-rich superberries to create a uniquely high-protein mix. In fact, just a ½-cup serving has 14 grams of protein. This trail mix is low-fat, too!

MAKES ABOUT 6 CUPS / 12 SERVINGS

2 cups dry-roasted and salted edamame

1 cup dried cranberries (juice-sweetened preferred)

1 cup dried goji berries

1 cup dried white mulberries

1 cup unsalted pepitas

Toss all the ingredients together in a bowl and store in a sealed container. Trail mix will keep for several months.

> **SUPERFOOD TIP:** You can find dry-roasted edamame in bulk bins in many supermarkets these days, or in the snack section of your local market. Choose a lightly salted variety if it's available, and most important, always choose organic or non-GMO certified soy products.

CHERRY QUINOA GRANOLA CLUSTERS

Big, chunky granola clusters are delicious, but often cloyingly sweet by my standards (and let's not even talk about the standard cup of oil with which they are often made— ew). This version is crunchy and craveworthy, yet much lighter thanks to all the flavorful natural ingredients. Toasting dry ingredients, such as quinoa seeds (remember quinoa is a seed, not a grain!) and flaxseeds before baking brings out a naturally nutty flavor.

MAKES 8 CUPS / 16 SERVINGS

1 teaspoon maca powder

1 teaspoon ground cinnamon

¼ teaspoon sea salt

1 cup rolled oats*

¼ cup uncooked quinoa

¼ cup flaxseeds

1 cup unsalted almonds, chopped

2 tablespoons coconut oil

⅓ cup maple syrup

½ cup crispy brown rice cereal

½ cup unsweetened dried cherries, chopped

*For gluten-free granola clusters, use gluten-free oats, available in natural food stores or online (see Resources Guide on page 209).

Preheat the oven to 300°F. Line a baking sheet with a silicone mat or parchment paper.

In a small bowl, mix together the maca powder, cinnamon, and sea salt; set aside. Heat a large sauté pan over medium heat. Add the oats, quinoa, flaxseeds, and almonds. Cook, stirring occasionally, until the oats are slightly golden and the almonds are fragrant, 5 to 6 minutes. Add the maca powder mixture and cook, stirring, for 1 minute longer. Add the coconut oil and stir to coat the ingredients. Pour in the maple syrup and cook, stirring constantly, until there is no excess syrup at the bottom of the pan. Remove from heat and stir in the rice cereal and cherries. Immediately transfer the hot granola to the prepared pan. Spread into a single layer across the surface of the pan, flatten with the back of a spatula, and bake for 20 to 25 minutes, or until granola is golden brown. Remove from the oven and let cool completely to harden. Break into large chunks, and serve. To store, transfer granola to an airtight container, where it will keep for several weeks.

Serving suggestions: *Sprinkle granola on top of smoothies and puddings, or stir into diced fruit or coconut yogurt; add almond milk (or milk of choice) and eat as a cereal; or enjoy a handful as a snack.*
Variation: *Use freeze-dried blueberries instead of (or in addition to) the dried cherries.*

SAVORY COCONUT CHIPS

You'll be amazed at how this simple recipe transforms normal coconut flakes (and dulse, for that matter) into the most craveable little crunchy chips that are almost bacon-like in flavor.

MAKES 1 CUP / 4 SERVINGS

2 tablespoons dulse flakes

1 cup unsweetened coconut flakes

1½ teaspoons yacon syrup or maple syrup

⅛ teaspoon smoked salt

Heat a sauté pan over medium heat. Add the dulse flakes and toast for 1 to 2 minutes, stirring frequently, until the dulse is fragrant and crispy but not burnt. Transfer the dulse flakes into a spice grinder or mortar and pestle and grind into smaller bits (some larger pieces will remain).

Return the empty pan to the stove and rewarm over medium heat. Have your ingredients, plus a stirring utensil and a medium bowl ready to go—quick action is important. Add the coconut flakes to the pan. Cook for 3 to 4 minutes, stirring frequently, until the flakes are toasted and range from golden to brown in color. Add the syrup and cook for 1 minute longer, stirring constantly. Quickly transfer the coconut to the bowl, add the dulse and salt, and mix very well to thoroughly combine and coat the coconut flakes. Let the mixture cool completely and crisp up, about 5 to 10 minutes. Stored in an airtight container, coconut chips will keep for several weeks at room temperature.

Serving suggestions: *Enjoy by the handful, or try a sprinkle over salads, potatoes, or on top of crostini, too.*

SUPERFOOD TIP: Make sure you use the right size of dried coconut! Coconut flakes are the larger strips of dried coconut that act like little "chips" in this recipe. Shredded dried coconut, on the other hand, is the smaller, almost confetti-like sprinkles (which are too small for this application).

CRANBERRY PISTACHIO BUCKWHEAT GRANOLA

I can barely keep my hands out of the granola jar after I've made this recipe. It has all the goodness of one of my favorite original granola flavors—cranberry orange—but the pistachios, buckwheat groats, and cacao nibs give it a grounding nuttiness that's beyond irresistible.

MAKES 8 CUPS / 16 SERVINGS

¼ cup ground flaxseed powder

½ cup fresh orange juice

1 teaspoon fresh orange zest

½ cup coconut sugar, divided

½ teaspoon sea salt

3 cups rolled oats*

1 cup buckwheat groats

¼ cup lucuma powder

1 cup shelled unsalted pistachios, chopped

1 cup dried cranberries (juice-sweetened preferred)

3 tablespoons cacao nibs (optional)

⅓ cup coconut oil, melted

2 tablespoons yacon syrup or maple syrup

*Gluten-free rolled oats may be used.

Preheat the oven to 350°F. Line a baking sheet with a silicone mat or parchment paper.

In a small bowl, combine the flaxseed powder, orange juice, orange zest, ¼ cup coconut sugar, and sea salt. Mix very well, and let sit for 15 minutes to form a gel.

In a large bowl, mix together the oats, buckwheat groats, lucuma powder, pistachios, cranberries, cacao nibs, and remaining ¼ cup coconut sugar. Stir the melted oil and the yacon syrup into the gelled flaxseed mixture, then pour the wet ingredients into the bowl of dry ingredients. Fold to combine.

Spread the mixture into an even layer on the prepared baking sheet, and use the back of spatula to flatten and compact. Bake for 15 minutes. Remove from the oven and use a spatula to flip over the granola in large chunks. Continue baking for 10 to 15 additional minutes, tossing the granola every few minutes, until it is crispy-looking and golden. Remove from the oven and let cool on the baking pan for several minutes (it will continue to get crunchier as it cools). When fully cooled, granola is ready to be enjoyed. To store, transfer granola to an airtight container, where it will keep for several weeks.

Serving suggestions: *Sprinkle granola on top of smoothies; stir into diced fruit or coconut yogurt; eat as a cereal; or just enjoy a handful.*

SPIRULINA SPICED PEPITAS

Savory with a little sweet 'n' smoky punch, these crunchy seeds have a whole lot of complex yum power.

MAKES ABOUT 2 CUPS / 4 SERVINGS

½ teaspoon cumin seeds

½ teaspoon pumpkin pie spice

¼ teaspoon chipotle powder

1 tablespoon coconut sugar

¼ teaspoon sea salt

1 tablespoon coconut oil

1 cup raw pumpkin seeds

¼ cup flaxseeds

2 tablespoons maple syrup

½ teaspoon spirulina powder

Add the cumin seeds to a sauté pan over medium heat and toast until fragrant for 2 to 3 minutes. Use a mortar and pestle (or spice grinder) to crush the cumin seeds into a powder. In a small bowl, mix together cumin powder, pumpkin pie spice, chipotle powder, coconut sugar, and sea salt.

In the same pan, warm the coconut oil over medium heat. Add the pumpkin seeds, and stir to coat with oil. Add the spice mix, stirring to distribute. Toast the seeds for 3 to 4 minutes, or until seeds swell slightly and begin to pop. Stir in the flaxseeds and toast for 30 seconds longer. Remove the pan from the heat and stir in the maple syrup. Once the syrup has stopped sizzling, sprinkle in the spirulina and stir very well. Transfer the contents to two large ceramic plates, and use the back of a spatula to spread the seeds into a thin layer. Let them cool for a minimum of 20 minutes—the seeds will be sticky at first, but they will harden as they cool. Store at room temperature for up to several weeks in a sealed airtight container.

Serving suggestions: *While these pepitas are an incredible snack to eat by the handful, you should also try them sprinkled on top of salads and roasted vegetables, or as a soup garnish.*

FEEL-GOOD FACT: Spirulina is a rich source of beta carotene: A 3 gram serving contains more than twice the beta carotene found in a carrot!

CRISPY GARBANZOS WITH NORI

Believe it or not, good things can come from indecision. One day, unable to decide between two snack favorites, toasted garbanzo beans and toasted nori sheets, the piggy voice in my head said, "why not have both?" And what do you know: high in protein, minerals, and fiber, this combo-snack is absolutely LOADED with savory munchie appeal. Plus, because it's fully stocked with nutrition, it will satisfy your hunger over the long run.

MAKES ABOUT 3 CUPS / 6 SERVINGS

2 15-ounce cans garbanzo beans (with salt)

1 tablespoon minced fresh rosemary

2 teaspoons chili powder

2 teaspoons sesame oil, divided

3 nori sheets

sea salt

Preheat the oven to 400°F.

Drain and rinse the garbanzo beans, and dry very well with a kitchen towel—the drier the beans, the crispier they will become. Place the beans in a bowl and add the rosemary, chili powder, and 1 teaspoon sesame oil, tossing to combine. Spread the beans onto a baking sheet in a single layer, and place in the center rack of the oven for 30 minutes. Remove from the oven and toss the beans, letting them cool for 5 minutes, while leaving the oven on for the nori.

While the beans are cooling, prepare the nori. Using a pastry brush or your fingers, lightly brush one side of a nori sheet with water. Sprinkle the sheet with sea salt, then fold it in half, pressing the damp sides together. Using kitchen scissors or a very sharp knife, cut the nori into 6 strips. Place them on the tray, on top of the beans. Repeat with the remaining nori.

Return the tray to the oven and bake for 10 to 15 minutes longer, until the beans begin to turn golden and the nori has warped and become crisp. Remove the tray from the oven, let it cool for a couple minutes, then crush the nori into bite-size pieces over the beans. Drizzle the beans and nori with the remaining 1 teaspoon sesame oil and toss well. Once fully cool, transfer to a bowl and serve. Best enjoyed immediately, for optimal crunch. Kept in a sealed container, this mix will last for up to 1 week.

AZTEC POPCORN

The ancient Aztecs can be described as pretty "way into" their corn—so much so that they created entire festivals around it. They were also way into a lot of what we now consider superfoods, such as chia seeds, cacao, and spices. This popcorn combines many of their favorite foods into one epic snack, and surprise, surprise: it's WAY GOOD.

MAKES ABOUT 5 CUPS / 2 SERVINGS

1 tablespoon cacao powder

2 teaspoons chia seeds

½ teaspoon ground cinnamon

Pinch cayenne pepper (big pinch for heat lovers)

Big pinch sea salt

2 tablespoons maple syrup

¼ teaspoon vanilla extract

2 tablespoons coconut oil, divided

¼ cup organic popcorn kernels

Set up the popcorn toppings in 3 small bowls first: In a small bowl mix together the cacao powder, chia seeds, cinnamon, cayenne, and sea salt. In a separate small bowl, mix the maple syrup and vanilla extract. Fill a third small bowl with 1 tablespoon of the coconut oil (solid state is okay). Have a large popcorn bowl ready.

Warm a large saucepan (3- to 4-quart size, with a lid) over medium-high heat and add the remaining tablespoon of coconut oil. Wait until the oil is hot, then add the popcorn. Stir to coat the kernels with oil, lightly shaking the pan to spread the kernels into a flat layer, then cover. Listen closely: once the first few kernels have popped, reduce the heat to slightly below medium (medium low–*ish*). Continue popping, placing the lid slightly ajar to release steam, and shaking the pan back and forth over the burner once every minute to ensure even cooking of the kernels. After 4 to 5 minutes, or once there are a couple seconds in between each pop, remove the popcorn from the heat. Uncover the popcorn and immediately add the remaining coconut oil, stirring quickly to distribute it. Drizzle in the maple syrup mixture over the surface of the popcorn and mix for 1 minute, stirring constantly, to help the maple syrup caramelize.

Transfer the popcorn to the large popcorn bowl. Sprinkle in the cacao-spice mixture a little at a time, tossing with your hands. This popcorn is best served warm, but it will keep in an airtight container for several days.

DULSE & PEPPER POPCORN

Dulse offers a briny, fresh-from-the-sea flavor and is a wonderful way to reduce salt. If you're really pressed for time or just craving savory popcorn ASAP (been there), simplify the directions by just tossing your popcorn with a little olive oil, dulse flakes, black pepper, and sea salt if you like. Still totally delicious.

MAKES ABOUT 5 CUPS / 2 SERVINGS

- 1½ tablespoons dulse flakes
- 1 teaspoon chia seeds (optional)

¼ teaspoon ground black pepper

⅛ teaspoon sea salt

⅛ teaspoon ground dried lemon peel

Pinch cayenne powder, to taste

1 recipe Basic Stovetop Popcorn (page 49)

1 tablespoon olive oil

½ lemon, cut into wedges (optional)

In a small bowl, mix together the dulse flakes, chia seeds, black pepper, sea salt, lemon peel, and a pinch of cayenne (use a large pinch if you like a lot of heat, and a small one if you like less heat). Place the prepared popcorn in a large bowl. Drizzle the popcorn with the oil, toss very well using your hands, and sprinkle the seasoning mixture a little at a time over the popcorn while tossing. For a tangier flavor, squeeze a little fresh lemon juice over the popcorn and toss again. This popcorn is best served fresh, but it will keep in an airtight container for several days.

SUPERFOOD TIP: Dried lemon peel is used instead of fresh in this recipe for its more delicate flavor as well as it's ability to better mix and adhere to the popcorn. You can purchase it wherever spices are sold, or you can make it yourself. For the homemade route, use a paring knife to cut off the peel of a lemon in strips. Place in a dehydrator overnight (or simply leave out at room temperature to dehydrate naturally for several days). Once hard, place in a spice grinder and blend into a powder. Store in an airtight container until ready to use.

BASIC STOVETOP POPCORN

Popcorn is a snack-food staple for me. While there's never a shortage of big puffy bags lining the store shelves, I still love making my own popcorn at home because it's so tremendously customizable—its mild flavor allows my spur-of-the-moment flavor musings to come to life, quickly and crunchily. I make my base recipe for popcorn extremely light in flavor, which makes turning it into superfood popcorn extra easy! Through diligent research making copious amounts of popcorn (it's a terrible job, I know), I've discovered that you need way less oil than most stovetop popcorn recipes call for, as long as you follow the recipe below closely.

MAKES ABOUT 5 CUPS / 2 SERVINGS

1 tablespoon grapeseed oil

¼ cup organic popcorn kernels

Warm a large saucepan (3- to 4-quart size, with a lid) over medium-high heat. Add the oil, wait until hot, then add the popcorn. Stir to coat the kernels with oil, lightly shake the pan to spread the kernels into a flat layer, then cover. Listen closely: once the first few kernels have popped, reduce the heat to just slightly below medium (medium low-*ish*). Continue popping, placing the lid slightly ajar to release steam, and shaking the pan back and forth over the burner once every minute to ensure even cooking of the kernels. After about 4 to 5 minutes, or once there are a couple seconds in between each pop, remove the popcorn from the heat and transfer to a bowl. Toss with superfoods and spices using one of the following recipes (Dulse and Pepper Popcorn or Aztec Popcorn), or add flavorings as desired.

CANDIED HEMP SEED CLUSTERS

Around the holidays, I like to give away jars filled with these clusters, which always earn rave reviews. Candied Hempseed Clusters are awesome to snack on out of the container, but they're so versatile you can use them to instantly enliven salads, oatmeal, and desserts. And, since this recipe includes not one, but two omega-3 powerhouse foods—hemp seeds and walnuts—they're a true "brain snack." (Although it's not likely you'll need any help remembering to eat them.)

MAKES ABOUT 2 CUPS / 4 SERVINGS

½ cup hemp seeds

½ teaspoon ground cinnamon

Pinch sea salt

3 tablespoons maple syrup

½ teaspoon vanilla extract

¼ teaspoon fresh orange zest

1 cup raw walnut halves

Line a baking sheet with a silicone mat or parchment paper.

In a small bowl, mix together hemp seeds and cinnamon with a pinch of salt, and set aside. In a separate small bowl, mix together the maple syrup, vanilla, and orange zest. Put both bowls near the stove for easy access during cooking.

Heat a sauté pan over medium heat and add the walnuts. Toast for 4 to 5 minutes, or until walnuts are fragrant. Add hemp seed mixture and continue to cook for a minute longer while stirring. Add the maple syrup mixture and cook for 2 minutes, stirring constantly. Transfer contents to the prepared baking sheet. Let the mixture cool entirely, then break it apart into clusters. Stored in an airtight container, clusters will keep for several weeks.

Variation: *Use pecans instead of the walnuts.*

MINI NORI ROLLS

The savory, mouthwatering, almost meaty flavor of these mini nori rolls shines through with every bite!

MAKES 2 DOZEN / 4 SERVINGS

- ⅓ cup hemp seeds
- ¼ cup raw sunflower seeds
- 1 tablespoon flaxseed powder
- 1 tablespoon nutritional yeast
- ¼ teaspoon dried oregano
- ¼ teaspoon onion powder
- ⅛ teaspoon garlic powder
- 1½ teaspoons yellow miso
- 1 tablespoon fresh lemon juice
- 3 nori sheets

Preheat the oven to 250°F.

In a food processor, combine all the ingredients, except the nori sheets, to make the filling. Pulse the ingredients until they're incorporated—the mixture should be well blended and stick together easily, yet retain a little bit of texture.

Using kitchen scissors or a very sharp knife, cut the nori sheets in half, lengthwise. Fill a small bowl with water. Place one nori half on a flat surface horizontally, and lightly paint the side facing up with water using a pastry brush. Spoon a thin line of the filling, 1½ tablespoons at a time, about 1 inch away from the horizontal edge. Use your fingers to roughly shape it into a line, then roll the seaweed upwards around the filling. Continue to roll upwards repeatedly in the same direction to smooth out the cylinder, as if creating a cigar, until the nori begins to shrink a little and sticks to its rolled shape easily. Dip your fingers in the water and lightly wet the edge of the roll, press, and seal. Set the roll aside on a plate, seal-side down, while you finish the remaining rolls. Once all rolls are complete, use a serrated knife to carefully cut each "cigar" into eights. Transfer all the mini rolls directly onto a baking sheet in a single layer. Bake on the center rack in the oven for 20 to 22 minutes, or until the filling has popped out of the sides of the seaweed, and the nori is dry. Transfer the mini rolls to a plate to cool, and serve.

Stored in sealed container, Mini Nori Rolls will keep at room temperature for approximately 1 week.

Variation: *Swap in different spices like chipotle or curry powder.*

SPOONABLES

Comforting the core, our visceral delight in eating spoon-foods starts in our very first years and never fully goes away . . . and why should it? Spoonables allow superfoods of all varieties to be folded in seamlessly within one of the most enjoyable of edible experiences. From puddings to parfaits to the best halved avocado of your life, the celebratory spoonables in this section shine with superfoods like immune-enhancing goji berries, anti-aging cacao, and brain-boosting chia seeds. Get your bowl and spoon ready; things are about to get good.

= FEATURED SUPERFOOD INGREDIENT

 BEAUTY   BONE STRENGTH   HEART HEALTH

 IMMUNITY   LOW CALORIE   PROTEIN

PAPAYA SMASH

Papaya is a funny fruit. Some people love it; others can't stand it. Obviously this is a recipe for lovers only, as papaya is really front and center here. Goji berries go amazingly well with this tropical, sensual fruit, and a little coconut helps make this snack a bit more well rounded. You can add in other fruits as well, such as chopped oranges and mangos.

MAKES 2¼ CUPS / 2 SERVINGS

2 cups fresh papaya (about ½ large fruit)

¼ cup dried goji berries

¼ cup shredded unsweetened coconut, plus more for garnish

2 tablespoons fresh lime juice

Freshly grated lime zest, for garnish (optional)

Scoop the papaya into a medium mixing bowl. With the back of a fork, mash the papaya into a chunky, juicy consistency—it doesn't have to be perfectly smooth. Mix in the goji berries, coconut, and lime juice. Refrigerate for a minimum of 30 minutes or up to several hours to allow the goji berries to rehydrate and absorb the excess papaya juice. To serve, garnish with coconut shreds and lime zest. If kept refrigerated, this delicious mixture will store for 2 to 3 days in a sealed container.

SUPERFOOD BOOST: Bump up the vitamin content and get additional antioxidants by mixing in a handful of dried goldenberries.

MANGO CHIA PUDDING

When you have a luscious recipe like this one, it's easy to understand why mango is one of the world's most popular fruits. Use super soft mangos, as the riper the fruit, the better the pudding.

MAKES 2 CUPS / 2 SERVINGS

2 large very ripe, soft mangoes

½ cup canned light coconut milk

1 tablespoon agave nectar

Liquid stevia

3 tablespoons chia seeds

Unsweetened coconut flakes or shreds, for serving (optional)

First, cut the fruit from the pit: Stand a mango on a cutting board, stem facing up. Holding the top of the mango with a steady hand, slice the two plump mango "cheeks" from the large inner pit on both sides. On each of the cheeks, lightly score the fruit flesh in a ½-inch wide crisscross pattern, taking care not to cut through the skin. Press the skin side inwards to invert and "pop" the mango chunks, and scoop them into a blender pitcher along with any fruit juices. Make a slice in the skin of the remaining piece of fruit that is still attached to the pit, and peel away the skin. If the mango is hard, slice away as much fruit from the pit as possible; if the mango is very soft and juicy, simply "milk" the pit over the blender pitcher by squeezing and pressing the flesh to get the juice out. Repeat with the remaining mango.

Add the coconut milk, agave nectar, and 6 drops of liquid stevia to the pitcher. Blend until smooth. Add the chia seeds and turn the blender on low for just a second to incorporate the chia seeds into the mixture, but do not blend. Taste for sweetness and mix in additional stevia, if needed. Pour the mixture into a bowl or sealable container and refrigerate for a minimum of 30 minutes to allow the chia seeds to swell and the pudding to thicken. To serve, divide the pudding into bowls and sprinkle with coconut.

SUPERFOOD BOOST: Add ¼ teaspoon of camu berry powder—that will more than double the vitamin C!

STRAWBERRIES & CREAM CHIA SWIRL

It's no secret that strawberries pair astonishingly well with cream, and here you get to enjoy this delicious flavor duo in the healthiest of ways!

MAKES 4 CUPS / 3 SERVINGS

2 cups unsweetened almond milk

2 tablespoons lucuma powder

1 teaspoon vanilla extract

1 teaspoon apple cider vinegar

1 teaspoon agave nectar

6 drops liquid stevia (or sweetener of choice, to taste)

Pinch sea salt

⅓ cup chia seeds

3 cups fresh strawberries, hulled and divided, plus extra for garnish

½ cup dried white mulberries

....

SUPERFOOD BOOST: Blend 1 teaspoon maqui berry powder into the strawberry mixture for extra antioxidant power.

....

In a blender, combine the almond milk, lucuma powder, vanilla extract, vinegar, agave nectar, stevia, and sea salt. Blend to combine. Add the chia seeds and turn the blender on low for just a second to incorporate the chia seeds into the mixture, but do not blend. Transfer the mixture to a large mason jar with a lid and refrigerate for 15 minutes, then shake the mixture well to redistribute the chia seeds. Refrigerate for a minimum of 20 minutes longer to allow the chia seeds to fully swell and create a thick mixture.

Meanwhile, add 2 cups of the strawberries to the blender and blend until liquefied. Toss in the mulberries and blend into a puree. Add the remaining cup of strawberries and blend just for a moment to lightly incorporate, leaving a few large chunks of fruit for texture. Refrigerate for a minimum of 15 minutes to let the mixture thicken slightly.

To assemble the dish, pour a couple tablespoons of the strawberry mixture into serving glasses or small bowls. Spoon a little of the chia mixture on top, and continue to layer, alternately, the strawberry and chia mixture. Use a knife to give the mixture a couple of decorative swirls, and top with fresh strawberries. You can also make one large "serving" in a mason jar using the same layering technique, and spoon out a portion whenever the mood strikes. This recipe will keep for several days, refrigerated.

CHOCOLATE PROTEIN CHIA PUDDING

Thanks to its high protein content (which comes from protein powder, chia seeds, and goji berries), high fiber, and generous minerals, this is a very sustaining, recharging snack. Chocolate Protein Chia Pudding is perfect for those times when you want something to keep you full and charged for a long time, without weighing you down. For best results, use the most delicious vanilla protein powder you can get your hands on (a couple of my personal favorites are listed in the Resource Guide on page 209). Depending on the brand you use, you may want to increase the sweetness by adding extra fruit or a little stevia.

MAKES 4 CUPS / 2–3 SERVINGS

3 cups coconut water

¼ cup soft Medjool dates (about 3–4), pits removed

¼ cup vanilla-flavored protein powder

3 tablespoons cacao powder

6 tablespoons chia seeds

3 tablespoons dried goji berries

Liquid stevia (optional)

Fresh fruit, for serving (optional)

In a blender, combine the coconut water, dates, protein powder, and cacao powder. Blend into a smooth cream. Add the chia seeds and goji berries and turn the blender on low for just a second to incorporate the ingredients, but do not blend. Transfer to a large mason jar with a lid and refrigerate for 15 minutes, then shake the mixture well to redistribute the chia seeds. Refrigerate for a minimum of 20 minutes longer to allow the chia seeds to fully swell and create a thick pudding. Since protein powders vary in flavor, taste and adjust the sweetness using stevia, if needed. Serve with your favorite fresh fruits, if desired. Pudding will keep for several days, refrigerated.

> **SUPERFOOD BOOST:** Make it green! Add 1 cup fresh baby spinach while blending the protein powder mixture with ¼ cup additional coconut water. Or, for a more undetectable green boost, simply add ½ teaspoon wheatgrass powder.

MACA, COCONUT, AND BLACK RICE PUDDING

Black rice brings a whole new arsenal of nutritional benefits to the world of rice pudding—in particular, the powerful anthocyanin antioxidants that give it its unique color. The delicious result is slightly more toothsome than conventional rice puddings, and the butterscotch-like maca flavor and copious health benefits are unsurpassed.

MAKES 3 CUPS / 3–4 SERVINGS

1 cup black rice

1 quart unsweetened almond milk

2 cups coconut water

⅓ cup maple sugar or coconut sugar

1 teaspoon vanilla extract

1 14-ounce can light coconut milk

2 tablespoons maca powder

Unsweetened coconut flakes (optional)

In a large saucepan, combine the rice with the almond milk, coconut water, maple sugar, and vanilla extract, and bring to a boil. Reduce heat to a simmer and cook for 40 minutes, stirring frequently, until the mixture has thickened. Combine the coconut milk and maca powder in a medium bowl, and whisk until fully incorporated. Add the mixture to the rice, bring to a simmer, and cook for 10 minutes longer, stirring occasionally, until rice is tender and the mixture is creamy. Remove from heat, let cool to room temperature, then refrigerate the pudding until it is well chilled, about 2 hours. Meanwhile, in a small sauté pan, toast the coconut over medium heat for 2 to 3 minutes or until fragrant and golden. Set aside to cool.

To serve, spoon the rice pudding into bowls and top with coconut flakes. Pudding will last for several days; store in an airtight container and refrigerate.

FEEL-GOOD FACT: Maca increases endurance and stamina, reduces stress and anxiety, and enhances overall well-being.

KRAUT-STUFFED AVOCADO BOAT

Mouthwatering. Maybe it's my Southern California roots finally marrying my eastern European heritage that make me crave this recipe pretty much all the time. (I'm not joking when I say that I eat this improbable avocado-and-kraut combo at least three times a week—it's one of my favorite snacks ever.) Plus, it's also extra fast to put together, filling, and nutritionally balanced. Perfect!

MAKES 2 AVOCADO HALVES / 2 SERVINGS

1 large avocado (such as Hass variety)

¼ cup sauerkraut or kimchi, drained

2 tablespoons hemp seeds

Ground cayenne pepper, to taste (optional)

Cut the avocado in half lengthwise, and extract the pit. Scoop out a very thin layer of avocado from each half—just to make the wells a little larger to hold more filling—but leaving most of the avocado intact. Place the avocado flesh you've removed into a small bowl. Add the sauerkraut and hemp seeds to the bowl, and mash them together. Spoon the filling back into the avocado, dividing it between both halves. Lightly dust them with cayenne pepper, if using. Serve immediately.

Variation: *Make kraut-avocado "taquitos." Here's how: Roughly mash all the ingredients together into a chunky mixture. Add in a handful of cubed firm organic tofu (optional), then roll the mixture, like a cigar, in sheets of nori, folding in the ends so the contents don't spill out. There are billions of other ways to customize this super simple recipe with additional vegetables and spices.*

APPLE PIE TEFF PORRIDGE

This teff porridge isn't just comfort food, it's what I call "mmmph" food, and it's definitely something to become friends with. I won't blame you if you take pains to savor every last teeny grain of this sweet and hearty caramel-colored concoction. With its homey suggestion of apple pie, it gives "gruel" a good name and is also loaded with minerals such as calcium and iron. After a few spoonfuls, you'll be on the energized go in no time.

MAKES APPROXIMATELY 4 CUPS / 4 SERVINGS

2 cups pure apple juice

¼ cup unsweetened almond milk, plus extra for serving

½ cup uncooked teff

½ teaspoon vanilla extract

1½ cups grated apples (about 2 medium apples)

⅓ cup raisins

1½ teaspoons ground cinnamon

2 tablespoons raw pecans, finely chopped

Pour the apple juice and ¼ cup almond milk into a medium-size saucepan, and bring to a boil. Reduce heat to medium-low, stir in teff and vanilla extract, and cover. Cook for 15 minutes, stirring occasionally. Uncover and mix in the apples, raisins, and cinnamon. Simmer for 5 to 6 minutes longer, uncovered, and stirring frequently until the teff is cooked through and any excess liquid has cooked away. Remove the mixture from the heat and let rest for 5 minutes.

Divide the porridge into bowls (or if storing for later, in four 6-ounce mason jars). Pour a little almond milk over each bowl—about 2 tablespoons each—and sprinkle with pecans. Enjoy the porridge warm, or seal in mason jars and refrigerate them to enjoy later. The porridge may be served cold or gently warmed up, and will last a few days, refrigerated.

SUPERFOOD BOOST: Sprinkle a dash of hemp seeds, flaxseeds, or chia seeds on top of the porridge to add some healthy omega fats.

EVERY BERRY SMOOTHIE BOWL

Well, almost "every berry" is in this smoothie bowl. In essence, it's a low-sugar cross between a smoothie and an acai bowl, with tons of berry varieties (including, yes, acai) mixed in, to offer a broader spectrum of antioxidants. You can make this wonderfully creamy, refreshing, and exceptionally energizing smoothie bowl in about the same amount of time it takes to prepare a bowl of cereal. If you really want to go to town, sprinkle the top with more fruit, cacao nibs, nuts, seeds, or even chopped herbs like mint or basil.

MAKES 1 BOWL / 1 SERVING

- 1 cup frozen mixed berries (raspberries, blackberries, etc.)

  ⅓ cup vanilla coconut yogurt or yogurt of your choice

  ⅓ cup unsweetened almond milk

- 1 tablespoon acai berry powder

- 2 tablespoons dried white mulberries

  1 teaspoon vanilla extract

- ½ cup of toppings (such as granola, fresh chopped fruit, dried berries, nuts and seeds, cacao nibs, mint or basil, etc.)

Blend the frozen berries, yogurt, almond milk, acai berry powder, dried mulberries, and vanilla extract until smooth. Pour the mixture into a serving bowl, and decorate with desired toppings. Serve immediately.

SUPERFOOD BOOST: Blend ¼ teaspoon of camu berry powder into the smoothie base for extra vitamin C, or use 1 teaspoon maqui berry powder in place of the acai berry powder. You can also incorporate some greens by blending in a handful of spinach leaves or ½ teaspoon wheatgrass powder, without ever tasting (or seeing) the difference.

SUPERFOOD-STYLE MUESLI

I think a better name for muesli would be "hodgepodge"—and this hodgepodge is composed of nothing but the best. Oats soaked overnight are wonderful—you just throw them into a jar with a few other things, and like magic, everything's perfectly soft, flavor-infused, and ready to go the next morning. Plus, by taking advantage of dried fruits and superfruits (which plump up right alongside their oat and quinoa-flake friends), you don't need to add any additional sugar. This muesli is a convenient, superfood-packed snack for any time of the day, and it keeps for several days in the fridge. It is a very swap-friendly recipe too, so feel free to substitute ingredients with any dried fruits, seeds, and nuts that you have on hand. You can also divide the recipe among small mason jars and top them with fruit for a grab-and-go snack.

MAKES 4 CUPS / 4 SERVINGS

1 cup rolled oats*

⅓ cup quinoa flakes

½ cup dried goji berries

¼ cup raisins

⅓ cup chia seeds

¼ cups hemp seeds

½ cup sunflower seeds

1½ cups apple juice

1 cup vanilla coconut yogurt or vanilla yogurt of your choice

Fresh fruit, for serving (optional)

Almond milk, for serving (optional)

*Gluten-free rolled oats may be used.

Mix together the oats, quinoa flakes, goji berries, raisins, and seeds in a large bowl. Once well combined, stir in the apple juice and yogurt. After the liquid is fully incorporated, transfer the mixture to mason jars or a sealable container and refrigerate overnight. Muesli may be served cold or gently warmed up. Top with fresh fruit, almond milk, or additional juice if desired. Muesli will keep for 2 to 3 days in the refrigerator.

Variation: *Use different types of juice to create new flavors. Mango juice, orange juice, and even pomegranate juice all create unique flavor twists.*

MAQUI PARFAIT
WITH POPPED AMARANTH

*Popped amaranth enhances recipes with a satisfying, nutty note without adding many calories.
I sprinkle it on just about anything—sweet or savory—for both a flavor and a protein boost.*

MAKES 2 PARFAITS / 2 SERVINGS

12 ounces unsweetened vanilla coconut yogurt, divided

1½ teaspoons maqui berry powder

Yacon syrup or maple syrup

1 cup fresh chopped fruit (such as peaches, plums, or mango)

3 tablespoons Popped Amaranth (recipe follows)

In a small bowl, whisk together 6 ounces of the yogurt with the maqui berry powder. Mix in a touch of syrup, to taste. If you're assembling the mix as a parfait, layer the maqui yogurt, vanilla yogurt, chopped fruit, and popped amaranth in small glass jars, and drizzle a little syrup over a couple of the layers in each to create a striped effect. Alternatively, divide the vanilla yogurt into bowls, spoon the maqui yogurt in the center, and scatter the fresh fruit, amaranth, and additional syrup on top.

POPPED AMARANTH

The first batch of popped amaranth can be a little tricky—you may need to slightly adjust the flame or temperature on your stove if the amaranth isn't popping quickly or if the grain is burning. The best advice is to have a very, very hot pan, or else the amaranth will not pop.

MAKES 2 CUPS

½ cup amaranth

Heat a large pot over very high heat—wait until the pot is very hot before you begin. Keep a bowl for the amaranth on standby.

Pour a tablespoon of the amaranth into the pot. The amaranth should begin to pop within a few seconds. Stirring constantly, let the amaranth pop as much as possible, and when the popping slows or the grains begin to brown, pour the amaranth into a bowl. Place the pot back on the stove, and repeat with the remaining amaranth, 1 tablespoon at a time. Store in an airtight container.

CRACKERS & CRISPS

The era of the empty calorie crunchy fix is over. Now, impressive mineral content, healthy fats, high fiber, and protein abound in these generously flavored, texturally rewarding homemade crackers and crisps. Superpower kale is sprinkled with spices and baked to a crisp, and grain-free crackers are composed of seeds like chia and flax, vegetables, and flavor-enhancing seaweed. These crave-worthy recipes are excellent for a midday munch that will offer a surprising level of satiety, energy, and long-term satisfaction.

 = FEATURED SUPERFOOD INGREDIENT

 BEAUTY BONE STRENGTH HEART HEALTH

 IMMUNITY LOW CALORIE PROTEIN

KETTLE KALE CRISPS

Kettle popcorn, meet your veggie-based match. These crisps are so sweet, salty, and crunchy, you'll never eat kale so quickly as with this recipe!

MAKES 4–6 CUPS / 2 SERVINGS

1 large bunch curly kale

1 tablespoon coconut oil, melted

2 tablespoons coconut sugar

½ teaspoon sea salt

Preheat the oven to 250°F. Line 2 baking sheets with silicone mats or parchment paper. You can also use the dehydrator method for this recipe (see page 39).

Strip kale leaves away from the stem one at a time and reserve the leaves in a large bowl. Tear any especially large pieces into halves or thirds. Toss the leaves with the coconut oil and massage them with your hands to ensure that the oil is well distributed. Sprinkle the leaves with coconut sugar and sea salt and toss well to distribute. Spread the leaves onto the prepared baking sheets and bake for 70 to 90 minutes, tossing once about an hour into baking, or until leaves are dry and crispy. Kale crisps may be stored in an airtight container for up to 2 weeks and may be recrisped by placing them in a 250°F oven for several minutes before serving.

FEEL-GOOD FACT: Gram for gram kale offers twice the vitamin C of oranges—the perfect nutrient compliment to make its impressive iron content more digestable.

TIPS FOR KALE CRISPS

Kale crisps are an ingenious way to get copious amounts of greens into your daily diet in the most delectable, snackable of ways (even kids love them)! Kale crisps can be a little fussy to make at first because they burn easily, but with these few tips, you'll be making best-ever batches in no time.

- ◆ Wash the kale thoroughly to remove any grit.
- ◆ Dry leaves very well—the drier the leaves, the faster they will cook!
- ◆ For best results, use curly kale. Its rumpled texture helps seasonings stick to the leaves. (Latigo, or "dinosaur" kale, can be used too.)
- ◆ Make chips out of the freshest, newest kale you can find. Don't use old kale that you've hung on to for too long, or else your chips will taste bitter.
- ◆ When you're preparing the pan, spread out the kale as evenly as possible, and undo any "clumps" to ensure even cooking.
- ◆ Check kale crisps frequently toward the end of cooking time—you may need to remove some crisps earlier than others. This is normal.
- ◆ Store kale crisps in an airtight container with a silica packet if you have one (you can reuse the silica packets that come with store-bought packages of seaweed and chips). You can also recrisp your kale by placing a batch in the oven at 250°F for just a couple minutes.

KALE & SEED CRISPS

*There's something about tahini (ground sesame seed paste) that just begs to be paired
with dark leafy greens—I always think of tahini as "grown-up" peanut butter.
Add a few textural seeds and spices to this recipe, and your protein, healthy fats,
complex carbs, and broad-spectrum micronutrients are just a crunch away.*

MAKES 4–6 CUPS / 2 SERVINGS

- 1 large bunch curly kale
- 2 tablespoons tahini (sesame seed paste)
- 1 tablespoon freshly squeezed lemon juice
- ½ teaspoon onion powder
- ¼ teaspoon smoked paprika powder
- ¼ teaspoon sea salt
- 2 tablespoons chia seeds
- 2 tablespoons sunflower seeds

Preheat the oven to 250°F. Line 2 baking sheets with silicone mats or parchment paper. You can also use the dehydrator method for this recipe (see page 39).

Strip the kale leaves away from the stems, and place them a large bowl. Tear any especially large leaves into halves or thirds.

In a small bowl, mix together the tahini and lemon juice. Stir in the spices and salt.

Pour the tahini mixture over the leaves and toss well, then add the seeds. Massage the kale by hand for a moment to ensure that the ingredients are well distributed. Spread the leaves onto the prepared baking sheets and bake for 70 to 90 minutes, tossing once after about an hour into baking, or until the leaves are dry and crispy. Kale crisps may be stored in an airtight container for up to 2 weeks and recrisped by placing them in a 250°F oven for several minutes before serving.

SUPERFOOD BOOST: Add a tablespoon of dulse flakes when mixing in the seeds and make this recipe even more of a mineral-rich powerhouse.

PIZZA KALE CRISPS

Not only do these crisps healthfully satisfy the urge to scarf down a slice, but while making them, your whole house will be suffused with the fabulous aromas of a pizzeria.

MAKES 4–6 CUPS / 2 SERVINGS

1 large bunch curly kale

¼ cup tomato paste

1 tablespoon yellow miso paste

1 teaspoon dried oregano

¾ teaspoon garlic powder

1 tablespoon dulse flakes (optional)

1 teaspoon agave nectar

¼ cup pine nuts

2 tablespoons hemp seeds

2 tablespoons nutritional yeast

Preheat the oven to 200°F. Line 2 baking sheets with silicone mats or parchment paper. You can also use the dehydrator method for this recipe (see page 39).

Strip the kale leaves away from the stem and place them in a large bowl. Tear any especially large leaves into halves or thirds.

In a small mixing bowl, use a fork to mash and mix together the tomato paste, miso paste, oregano, garlic powder, dulse flakes, and agave. Add the tomato mixture to the kale and use your hands to gently massage and distribute it evenly among the leaves.

In a blender or food processor on high speed, briefly pulverize the pine nuts, hemp seeds, and nutritional yeast into a powder. Crumble the mixture over the kale, then gently hand toss the leaves to distribute the mixture evenly, leaving a few "clusters" of the pine nut mixture amongst the leaves to create a "cheesy" look.

Spread the leaves onto the prepared baking sheets and bake for 70 to 90 minutes, tossing once, after about an hour into baking, or until the leaves are dry and crispy. Kale crisps may be stored in an airtight container for up to 2 weeks and recrisped by placing them in a 250°F oven for several minutes before serving.

SUPERFOOD BOOST: Add ¼ teaspoon turmeric plus ¼ teaspoon camu berry powder to the spice mixture to boost the anti-inflammatory benefits of the kale crisps.

CURRIED COCONUT KALE CRISPS

If you are searching for an extra-extra simple kale crisp recipe with lots of flavor, look no further. Truth be told, even before cooking it, the kale in this recipe is so delicious that I sometimes just end up eating it raw—it's an incredible salad! But snacks are our cookbook subject matter here, so for now, let's get crispy . . .

MAKES 4–6 CUPS / 2 SERVINGS

1 large bunch curly kale or Latigo kale

¼ cup coconut butter

½ tablespoon curry powder

¼ teaspoon sea salt

Preheat the oven to 200°F. Line 2 baking sheets with silicone mats or parchment paper. You can also use the dehydrator method for this recipe (see page 39).

Strip the kale leaves away from the stems, and place them in a large bowl. Tear any especially large leaves into halves or thirds.

In a small saucepan, melt the coconut butter into a liquid over moderate heat. Whisk in the curry powder and sea salt.

Pour the coconut mixture over the leaves and toss well, massaging them by hand to ensure that the ingredients are well distributed. Spread the leaves onto the prepared baking sheets and bake for 70 to 90 minutes, tossing once after about an hour into baking, or until the leaves are dry and crispy. Kale crisps may be stored in an airtight container for up to 2 weeks and recrisped by placing them in a 250°F oven for several minutes before serving.

Variation: *Make it spicy! Add ⅛ teaspoon cayenne powder (or more!) along with the curry to amplify the heat.*

BRUSSELS SPROUTS & PINE NUT CRISPS

This recipe is like the muffin-top of the vegetable world. Anyone who's roasted Brussels sprouts before knows how utterly magnificent their earthiness is . . . and that the best part is the extra-crisp leaves on the outside. So, to be utterly indulgent, here's how to get a whole pan of nothing but those choice pieces.

MAKES 4 CUPS / 4 SERVINGS

- 1 pound Brussels sprouts
- 1 tablespoon olive oil
- ¼ cup raw pine nuts
- 2 tablespoons hemp seeds
- ⅓ cup nutritional yeast
- ½ teaspoon sea salt

Preheat the oven to 400°F. Line 2 baking sheets with silicone mats or parchment paper.

Slice away the tough end off of the Brussels sprouts. Peel off and reserve the large leaves, and discard the core. In a large bowl, toss the leaves with the olive oil.

In a food processor or blender, blitz the pine nuts, hemp seeds, nutritional yeast, and sea salt into a rough powder. Sprinkle the mixture over the Brussels sprouts and toss to coat evenly. Spread the leaves onto the baking sheets and bake for 10 to 12 minutes, tossing once halfway through, or until leaves are browned and crispy.

For the crispiest results, enjoy the roasted Brussels sprouts within an hour, before the leaves begin to soften. To recrisp the leaves, place them in a 250°F oven for several minutes before serving.

FEEL-GOOD FACT: Researchers in the Netherlands discovered that habitually eating Brussels sprouts led to an incredible 28 percent reduction in DNA damage, the mutations that make cancer cells develop. Clearly Brussels sprouts are an excellent kitchen tool for cancer prevention!

TOASTED HEMP SEED NORI CRISPS

For years I'd see 50-count packages of nori in the store and think to myself, "who on earth would need that much seaweed?" Well, my friends, my new theory is: the nori crisp makers of the world. WOW does this snack get chomped up fast. Although this recipe shows off my favorite flavor combination (if you use the walnut oil), the variations are endless once you master the basic method. Spice rack, I'm looking at you.

MAKES 5 DOZEN CRISPS / 5 SERVINGS

6 sheets untoasted nori

1 tablespoon walnut oil or sesame oil

Sea salt (optional)

¼ cup hemp seeds

FEEL-GOOD FACT: Nori's mineral content alone accounts for up to 40% of its dry mass—talk about nutrient-dense!

Preheat the oven to 250°F. Line 2 baking sheets with silicone mats or parchment paper. With a pair of kitchen scissors or a sharp knife, cut each of the nori sheets in half lengthwise.

Pour the oil in a small bowl. In a separate bowl, pour a little water. Work one at a time with the nori sheet halves: Using a pastry brush, lightly coat the dull side of the nori with a minimal amount of oil. Lightly brush the sheet again with water, using the same method—you may also use a spray bottle for this step. Lightly dust the sheets with sea salt and then scatter some hemp seeds over them (they'll stick to the oil). Carefully cut the nori into strips and transfer to a baking sheet. Repeat with remaining nori sheets—the strips may touch one another on the baking sheet, but should be in a single layer without overlapping.

Bake the nori for 18 to 20 minutes or until nori has darkened, buckled, and become brittle. Remove the nori strips from the oven and let them cool to room temperature. Enjoy them immediately, and store leftover nori strips in an airtight container. They will keep for several days; to recrisp the nori strips, place them in a 250°F oven for several minutes before serving.

CHIA THINS

These chia thins taste (and look) a lot like wheat thins, but they are gluten free, protein rich, and offer a wonderful flavor and crunch. I love them because they are the type of cracker that truly satisfies for long periods of time—as opposed to most crackers, which leave you yearning for something more!

MAKES 4 DOZEN / 8 SERVINGS

2¼ cups almond flour

½ cup chia seeds

1 cup chopped celery

¼ cup water

1 tablespoon olive oil

1 tablespoon yellow miso paste

Flaked or regular sea salt (optional)

Preheat the oven to 350°F. You can also use the dehydrator method for this recipe (see page 39).

In a large bowl, mix together the almond flour and chia seeds.

In a blender, combine the celery, water, olive oil, and miso paste. Blend until smooth. Pour the mixture into the bowl with the chia and flour, and mix well. Knead the mixture by hand for 1 to 2 minutes to help compact it, then form the dough into two compact logs. Lay a silicone mat (or parchment paper) on a baking sheet, and place one log on top. Lightly grease a rolling pin, and roll the log out flat to cover the whole surface of the baking sheet, leaving just 1-inch from all sides (dough should be about ⅛-inch thick). Lightly sprinkle with sea salt, and use a pizza cutter or sharp knife to score the dough into 2-inch squares. Repeat with the remaining dough on a separate baking sheet. Bake in the center rack of the oven for 18 to 22 minutes, or until the crackers are golden. Cool on the baking sheets before snapping into the pre-scored squares. Stored in a sealed container, crackers will last several weeks.

> **FEEL-GOOD FACT:** Chia seeds are a natural appetite suppressant thanks to their healthy fats and fiber. In fact, ounce per ounce these little seeds have more omega-3 fatty acids than salmon and more fiber (but fewer carbs) than rice and grains!

4 TIPS FOR GREAT HOMEMADE CRACKERS

1. Don't just roll out the dough thinly, roll it out evenly. Spend extra time rolling your dough as flatly as possible before baking to ensure even cooking.

2. Always bake on the center racks, and rotate the pan halfway through baking.

3. Since crackers can burn easily, keep a close eye on them towards the end of cooking time so you can pull them out when they turn golden brown. If the edges are baked before the center, pull them off the pan to cool, and return the remaining crackers to the oven to finish cooking.

4. Keep your crackers crisp by storing in an airtight container with a silicone packet (you can reuse them from other packaged snacks). To re-crisp crackers that have gone soft, place them in a 250°F oven for a couple minutes.

AMARANTH CHIPS

These delectable gluten-free crisps are incredibly light, yet they can still stand up to a dip. Made from 100% superfoods, they are full of protein, packed with fiber, and offer an excellent supply of minerals—especially iron, calcium, and phosphorus.

MAKES 3 DOZEN / 6 SERVINGS

- ½ cup uncooked amaranth
  1½ cups water
- 3 tablespoons chia seeds
  ½ teaspoon sea salt

Combine the amaranth and water in a saucepan. Cover and bring to a boil on the stovetop. Reduce heat to a simmer and cook, stirring occasionally, for 25 minutes or until all the excess water is absorbed, and the grains have formed a sticky, thick porridge. Remove the mixture from heat and transfer it to a bowl. Add chia seeds and sea salt, mix well, and let cool to room temperature, about 20 minutes.

Heat the oven to 325°F. Place a silicone baking mat* on a flat surface. Scoop and shape the dough into teaspoon-size balls, and place them a few inches apart on the mat—1 dozen balls per sheet. Cover the balls with a second silicone baking mat* and, using a rolling pin, roll the balls into thin discs, about 3 inches in diameter. A perfect circle is not as important as getting the crisps perfectly flat, so take care to roll them out into a truly even layer, otherwise the crisps will cook at unpredictable rates. Still sandwiched between the mats, transfer the discs to a baking sheet, then slowly peel away the top mat. Repeat with the remaining dough to yield 3 baking sheets total (you can also bake the chips one batch at a time if you prefer). Bake the chips for 20 to 24 minutes, rotating the pans hallway through. Chips are done when they are golden, completely dried out, and begin to curl up at the edges. Remove the pans from from the oven and use a spatula to transfer the crackers to a wire rack until cool. The chips may be stored in a sealed container or bag for several weeks.

*You can also use parchment paper that has been sprayed lightly with oil on the side that will have contact with the dough.

GREEN CRACKERS

*Thanks to high amounts of fiber, protein, healthy fats and, as the name suggests, greens,
you'll find these mouthwatering crackers function almost like a mini meal.*

MAKES 4 DOZEN / 12 SERVINGS

2 cups cashews

⅔ cup ground flaxseed powder

⅔ cup coconut flour

1½ tablespoons nutritional yeast

½ teaspoon baking soda

2 tablespoon coconut oil

2 tablespoons miso paste

1½ cup packed spinach,
chopped fine

¼ cup fresh parsley, minced

¼ cup fresh chives, minced

1 tablespoon fresh lemon juice

3–4 tablespoons water

flaked or regular sea salt
(optional)

Preheat the oven to 350°F. You can also use the dehydrator method for this recipe (see page 39).

In a food processor, grind the cashews into a fine flour. Add the flaxseed powder, coconut flour, nutritional yeast and baking soda and blend. Add the coconut oil, miso paste, spinach, parsley, chives, lemon juice, and 3 tablespoons of water. Process until the greens are blended. Stop the machine and check the consistency of the dough—it should stick together easily and feel pliable. If dough is too dry, mix in additional water, a teaspoon at a time. Remove the dough from the machine, divide into halves, and compact each half into a log. Let the dough rest for 10 minutes.

Grease a rolling pin with oil. Place 1 of the logs onto a silicone baking mat or parchment paper, and roll out to cover the entire surface of the mat. Using a pizza cutter or sharp knife, slice away the rough edges, and score into 24 squares. Repeat with the second log on a separate baking sheet. If desired, lightly sprinkle the surface with salt. Bake the 2 sheets for 10 minutes on the center rack, then carefully flip the crackers with a spatula. Continue to bake for 5 to 10 minutes longer, or until light brown. Carefully transfer large sections of the crackers (they will partially stick together) to a baking rack to cool. Once the crackers are fully cool and have hardened, snap into the pre-scored squares. Stored in a sealed container, crackers will last several weeks.

SUNFLOWER DULSE CRACKERS

Far from a boring cracker, these protein-rich beauties offer a well-seasoned savory crunch that hints at the flavor of teriyaki.

MAKES 4 DOZEN / 12 SERVINGS

1½ cups sunflower seeds

½ cup coconut flour

½ cup ground flaxseed powder

½ teaspoon baking soda

½ cup red onion, minced

3 tablespoons fresh ginger, peeled and minced

2 tablespoons olive oil

2 tablespoons yellow miso paste

3–4 tablespoons water

2 tablespoons dulse flakes

2 tablespoons sesame seeds, plus extra for garnish

Preheat the oven to 325°F. You can also use the dehydrator method for this recipe (see page 39).

Place the sunflower seeds in a food processor, and grind into a fine flour. Add the coconut flour, flax powder, and baking soda and pulse to combine. Add the onion, ginger, olive oil, miso and 3 tablespoons of water, and process until the minced vegetables are fully ground down and a dough has formed. Stop the machine and check the consistency of the dough—it should stick together easily and feel pliable without being wet. If dough is too dry, mix in additional water, a teaspoon at a time, until a compact dough is achieved. Add the dulse and 2 tablespoons of sesame seeds, and mix briefly to combine, while leaving the texture of the added ingredients intact. Remove the dough from the machine, divide into thirds, and compact each third into a log. Let the dough rest for 10 minutes.

Grease a rolling pin with oil. Place 1 of the logs onto a silicone baking mat or parchment paper on a flat surface, and roll out to cover the entire surface of the mat, up to 1-inch away from the edges. Using a pizza cutter or sharp knife, slice away the rough edges, and score into 24 squares. Repeat with the remaining log on a separate baking sheet. Bake the 2 sheets for 12 minutes, then remove from the oven and use a spatula to carefully flip the crackers over. Return to the oven and continue to bake for 5 to 10 minutes longer, or until golden. Allow the crackers to fully cool and harden on the baking sheets, then snap them into the pre-scored squares. Stored in a sealed container, crackers will last several weeks.

SPREADS & DIPS

Ranging from silky and smooth to peppery and feisty, spreads and dips come in all kinds of wondrous and complex flavors. A mostly uncooked category, this is an ideal spot to include superfoods of all varieties, like superstar spirulina, vitamin C king camu, and mouthwatering Omega-rich hemp seeds. Healthy bases like beans, avocado, and nuts round out the recipes, ensuring no ingredient is wasted from a nutritional standpoint. Profoundly versatile, a great superfood spread can revitalize just about anything — from crudités to crackers to toast.

= FEATURED SUPERFOOD INGREDIENT

 BEAUTY ● BONE STRENGTH ♥ HEART HEALTH

 IMMUNITY ◊ LOW CALORIE ⬡ PROTEIN

RUSTIC CHIA GUACAMOLE

This is an extra-exciting guacamole, which says a lot because, by most people's standards, guacamole is already pretty exciting. Yet, in addition to skin-healthy fats, this recipe also offers a significant serving of important minerals, thanks to some sneaky fresh greens, gelled chia seeds (which could almost pass as tomato seeds in terms of texture) and dulse flakes, which add an irresistible, nonstop savory flavor boost.

MAKES APPROXIMATELY 2 CUPS / 8 SERVINGS

1 extra large juicy tomato (or 2 medium), heirloom variety preferred

2 tablespoons chia seeds

1½ large avocados, pitted, peeled, and chopped

1½ cups baby spinach leaves, minced very fine

2 heaping tablespoons minced fresh cilantro, plus extra leaves for garnish

2 tablespoons fresh lime juice

1 teaspoon Sriracha sauce

2 scallions, white and light green parts, minced

1 tablespoon dulse flakes, plus extra for garnish

¼ teaspoon sea salt, plus extra to taste

¼ cup heirloom cherry tomatoes, halved, for garnish (optional)

Slice the tomato in half. Use a spoon to scoop out the seeds and juicy interior into a food processor, setting aside the fleshy tomato shell. Blend the tomato seeds and juice into a puree and transfer to a cup or small bowl. Add the chia seeds and stir well. Let the mixture sit for 10 minutes, allowing the chia seeds to swell.

While the chia mixture is thickening, place the avocados in a bowl and mash with a fork to rough up the chopped pieces, while still leaving plenty of texture. Add the minced spinach and cilantro, lime juice, Sriracha sauce, scallions, dulse flakes, and sea salt, and mix well. Finely chop the tomato shell, and add it to the guacamole bowl. Pour the chia seed mixture into the bowl and mix until all ingredients are well distributed and a chunky dip has formed. Taste, and adjust seasoning as desired. Transfer to a serving bowl and garnish with cherry tomatoes, extra cilantro, and a light sprinkle of dulse flakes and sea salt. This guacamole will keep in the refrigerator for several days.

Serving suggestions: *Enjoy the dip with sliced vegetables such as jicama or celery, or enjoy it on chips, crisps, and toast, or inside a wrap.*

FEEL-GOOD FACT: A single avocado has the potassium of 3 bananas, without the sugar!

GOJI WALNUT HUMMUS

So often goji berries are reserved just for sweets, but this slightly spicy hummus is a great example of just how delicious they can be in savory applications too. If you're using salted garbanzo beans, omit the salt or add as needed after blending the hummus into a smooth mixture.

MAKES 2 CUPS / 8 SERVINGS

¼ cup dried goji berries, plus additional for garnish

2 cups unsalted canned garbanzo beans

⅓ cup raw walnuts

2 tablespoons olive oil

3 tablespoons fresh lemon juice

1 teaspoon chili powder, or more to taste

⅛ teaspoon cayenne pepper

½ teaspoon sea salt

FEEL-GOOD FACT: Eating a handful of walnuts daily has been shown to reduce cholesterol, and enhance the functioning of blood vessels.

Place the goji berries in a cup and mix with a little water—just enough to cover by 1 to 2 inches. Let them sit for 15 minutes to soften. Gently drain the water, taking care not to squish the plumped berries.

In a food processor, combine the remaining ingredients and process for a couple minutes, until the mixture is very smooth and free of clumps. If needed, stop the machine and scrape down the sides with a silicone spatula to ensure all ingredients are fully incorporated. When the hummus is fully whipped and creamy, stop the machine and add the goji berries. Pulse the machine a couple times—just long enough to chop some of the berries while keeping some large bits intact, for texture and color.

Transfer the hummus to a serving bowl or plate. Garnish with a few goji berries. You can also sprinkle a little extra chili powder, drizzle some olive oil, or scatter a few chopped walnuts and additional garbanzo beans over the top. The hummus will keep for up to 1 week in a covered container in the refrigerator.

Serving suggestions: *Vegetables such as carrots and jicama are ideal for this dip, or use it as a spread for rice cakes, sandwiches, or wraps.*

WASABI EDAMAME HUMMUS

High-protein edamame replaces the go-to garbanzo bean in this VERY addictive green hummus, which relies more on the enticing flavor of wasabi than on its notorious heat. And, although spirulina enhances the color of the hummus and adds hyper-condensed nutrition, you'll find the taste of this green powder goes unnoticed. Even though it has a fancy superfood pedigree, this recipe can be used just like any other typical hummus and is particularly outstanding on brown rice cakes and rice crackers.

MAKES 2 CUPS / 8 SERVINGS

2 cups unsalted shelled edamame, cooked and cooled

2 tablespoons tahini

3 tablespoons hemp seed oil or olive oil

¼ cup fresh lemon juice

1 tablespoon yellow miso paste

½ teaspoon spirulina powder

½ teaspoon garlic powder

¼ teaspoon onion powder

½ teaspoon sea salt

1 teaspoon wasabi powder

⅓ cup fresh chopped parsley, plus additional for garnish

1 nori sheet, crushed into small flakes (optional, for garnish)

Combine all the ingredients in a food processor and blend until very smooth and creamy. Mix in a little water, about 2 to 3 tablespoons, to lighten the hummus. Refrigerate for 10 minutes to allow the flavor of the wasabi to develop. Transfer the mixture to a serving bowl or plate and garnish with additional parsley and nori flakes, if desired. The hummus will keep for up to 1 week in the fridge in a covered container.

Serving suggestions: *Enjoy Wasabi Edamame Hummus with rice cakes, rice crackers, sliced veggies such as cucumber and carrots, and warm pita wedges.*

SUPERFOOD TIP: Making Wasabi Edamame Hummus is effortless if you use frozen shelled edamame, which can easily be thawed in the refrigerator—ready to use! As with any soy product, be sure to purchase organic and/or non-GMO certified edamame.

POMEGRANATE SALSA

Tart and sweet, savory and fresh, this exquisitely uncommon superfood salsa is hard to put down.

MAKES 1½ CUPS / 4 SERVINGS

3 tablespoons minced shallots

1 tablespoon fresh lemon juice

¼ teaspoon sea salt

1 cup fresh pomegranate seeds (about 1 large pomegranate)

⅓ cup finely diced cucumber

1 tablespoon olive oil

1 tablespoon yacon syrup or agave nectar

2 heaping tablespoons chopped mint, tough stems discarded

2 heaping tablespoons chopped cilantro

Combine the shallots, lemon juice, and salt in a medium mixing bowl and toss together. Let the mixture stand for 5 minutes, then add the remaining ingredients and mix well. For best results, refrigerate for a minimum of 10 minutes prior to serving to allow the flavors to meld. Store the salsa in a sealed container in the refrigerator, where it will keep for a few days.

Serving suggestions: *Enjoy Pomegranate Salsa with chips or flatbread, tucked inside of a lettuce or endive leaf, or tossed over a batch of premade quinoa with a few chopped walnuts or almonds sprinkled on top.*

SUPERFOOD BOOST: Mix in 1 tablespoon chia seeds, which will not only soak up the flavorful excess juices, but will also make this light snack a little more filling thanks to the high fiber content of chia.

CAULIFLOWER RANCH DIP

This is a low-fat, low-calorie, dairy-free ranch dip that is sure to please even the most devoted ranch lover. It goes great with vegetables, especially broccoli florets; in fact I've been known to eat an entire crown of broccoli so long as it's accompanied by this dip!

MAKES 1½ CUPS / 6 SERVINGS

1½ cups steamed cauliflower florets*

½ cup unflavored almond milk

2 tablespoons grapeseed oil

2 tablespoons apple cider vinegar

2 tablespoons hemp seeds

½ teaspoon Dijon mustard

¼ teaspoon garlic powder

Shot of hot sauce, to taste

½ teaspoon sea salt

¼ teaspoon freshly ground black pepper

2 tablespoons fresh chives, minced

*You can also use frozen cauliflower that has been thoroughly defrosted.

Place the cauliflower in a blender, along with the almond milk, grapeseed oil, apple cider vinegar, and hemp seeds. Blend for a full minute, or until completely smooth and creamy. Add the Dijon mustard, garlic powder, hot sauce, along with the sea salt and black pepper, then blend to combine. Taste and adjust salt and pepper if needed. Add the chives and blend briefly just to incorporate, without processing the chives too much. Transfer the dip to a serving bowl or a resealable container, and refrigerate for 1 hour to chill before serving. It will keep, refrigerated, for 1 week.

Serving suggestions: *This dip is especially good with fresh vegetables, particularly broccoli and carrots. It may also be enjoyed with roasted sweet potato fries or roasted carrots.*

FEEL-GOOD FACT: Cauliflower is an astonishingly good source of vitamin K: 1 cup has a whopping 476.2 % of the RDA! People with higher levels of vitamin K have greater bone density and a lower rate of osteoporosis.

HOT CREAMY KALE DIP

It's a dip . . . it's a spread . . . it's a bowl of something you desperately try not to devour in a single sitting (alas, I project). This amazing, can't-stop-eating-it dip is perfect for parties or just a midday munch. You can serve it with small toasts or crudités—or put it in a ceramic serving bowl and keep it warm in a low-temperature oven until you're ready to serve. Leftovers are also delicious cold, though it's unlikely there will be any.

MAKES 2 CUPS / 8 SERVINGS

½ cup raw cashews

1 tablespoon yellow miso paste

½ cup water

1 tablespoon olive oil

1 cup finely chopped yellow onion

½ teaspoon ground cumin

pinch cayenne pepper

6 cups packed curly kale leaves, finely chopped

Sea salt

2 tablespoons fresh lemon juice

1 tablespoon nutritional yeast

¼ cup hemp seeds, plus additional for garnish

Place the cashews, miso paste, and water in a blender and blend until the mixture is as smooth as possible.

Heat the oil in a large pan over medium-high heat. Add the onion and sauté for 3 to 4 minutes, or until onions are softened and translucent. Add the cumin, cayenne, kale, and a big pinch of salt and cook, stirring constantly, for about 1 minute or until kale is wilted to about half its original size and bright green. Reduce the heat to medium-low and pour in the cashew mixture (don't clean the blender—you'll be adding ingredients back into it shortly). Cook the mixture for 3 to 4 minutes longer, stirring constantly to prevent burning. Remove from heat and spoon the kale back into the blender. Add the lemon juice, nutritional yeast, and hemp seeds, and blend to partially puree while still leaving small textural bits of the vegetables intact. (You will likely need to stop the blender several times and manually stir the ingredients back down toward the blades before blending again.) Taste the dip, add additional salt as needed, then serve.

Serving suggestions: *Use this dip as a spread for toast or crackers, brown rice cakes, or wrapped in a sprouted tortilla.*

AVOCADO NORI CROSTINI

There is only one thing that is better than creamy avocado on toast, and that's creamy avocado on toast with just a teeny touch of buttery coconut oil. And there's only one thing better than THAT . . . which, my friend, is this recipe. While it is pretty epic fare for entertaining, you can also prepare it family-style if you slather the whole piece of toast with avocado goodness (transforming it into the best-ever half-sandwich), instead of quartering it into bite-size pieces.

MAKES 16 CROSTINI / 4 SERVINGS

2 nori sheets

½ cup mashed avocado (about 1 large)

½ teaspoon fresh lemon juice

¼ teaspoon sea salt

4 slices sprouted-grain bread*

1 tablespoon coconut oil

1 tablespoon chia seeds

¼ cup chopped raw walnuts

*Note: Sprouted-grain bread, which is now available at many natural food stores, has a pleasant, lightly nutty flavor and is particularly beneficial, thanks to its naturally higher protein content. Of course, you can also use any bread you like, or for more traditional crostini, use thick slices of a toasted baguette instead.

Over a wide bowl, crumple one sheet of nori into the smallest flakes possible. Repeat with remaining nori sheet.

In a small mixing bowl, combine the avocado, lemon juice, and sea salt. Mix well. Add half of the crushed nori flakes and fold them gently into the mixture to combine.

Toast the bread in a toaster or oven broiler for 1 to 2 minutes on each side, until golden. Lightly brush one side of each piece of toast with coconut oil and cut it into quarters. Spread each quarter with a spoonful of avocado mixture, then sprinkle with chia seeds, remaining nori flakes, and walnuts. Plate and serve.

BASIC SUPERFOOD CHEESE

Artisanal yet homey, there is something deeply satisfying about making your own "cheese" from nature's transformational fats: nuts and seeds. While nondairy cheeses do share many of the same flavor notes (creamy, tangy, indulgent) as conventional dairy cheeses, they offer their own nuances (plus are cholesterol free, rich in omega fatty acids, protein, minerals, and more.) For an easy riff on this main recipe, try all of the variations on the following pages, too!

Note: You can use other types of nuts, such as cashews or Brazil nuts, in place of macadamias, and still get good results. However, macadamias create the best texture—almost like a soft chevre—for this method.

MAKES 4 ROUNDS / 16 SERVINGS

2 cups macadamia nuts

¼ cup hemp seeds

1¼ cups water

1 teaspoon probiotic powder*

1 tablespoon nutritional yeast

¾ teaspoon sea salt

1 teaspoon fresh lemon juice

*Simply open probiotics capsules and empty the powder into a small bowl—a teaspoon is usually equivalent to 6 to 8 capsules. Probiotics are friendly bacteria that are often taken as a health supplement. The powder is used here as the "starter" for culturing the nuts that will improve the cheese's flavor and texture. After you're finished making cheese, keep the remaining probiotics, and take them according to the manufacturer's directions, as a way to boost your immune system and increase nutrient absorption—they are one of the most beneficial supplements to have on hand!

Place the macadamia nuts in a bowl and add enough water to cover them by an inch. Refrigerate and let the nuts sit for a minimum of 4 hours up to overnight to soften and slightly swell.

Drain the nuts and place in a blender. Add the hemp seeds, water, and probiotic powder. Blend until very smooth, stopping the blender and scraping down the sides as needed—this process may take a few minutes to blend the mixture into a super-smooth consistency. If needed, add a little more water (up to ¼ cup) just to get the mixture blending—the less water you use, the better.

Put two 12-inch square layers of cheesecloth (or use a nut-milk bag—see the Resources Guide on page 209 for sourcing) inside a colander. Place the colander inside a large bowl or tray to catch excess liquid. Use a silicone spatula to scrape all of the nut mixture from the blender into the center of the cheesecloth. Gather up the ends of the fabric to create a bag, hold it over the bowl, and gently squeeze all of the mixture in a downward motion into a ball at the bottom of the bag. Squeeze the cheese ball lightly to encourage excess milky liquid to be pushed through the cheesecloth, but not too hard, or else the nuts will begin to push through the cloth as well. Twist the ends of the cheesecloth together to wrap snugly around the cheese ball and set it inside the colander. Place a heavy weight—such as a water-filled mason jar placed in a small pot—on top of the cheese. Cover the whole thing with a towel, and let it rest at room temperature for 24–48 hours.

Peel away the cheesecloth, and place the cheese inside of a bowl. Add nutritional yeast, sea salt, and lemon, and mix to combine. Taste and adjust seasoning, if desired. Put one-fourth of the cheese mixture onto a piece of plastic wrap and shape it into a 4-inch compact cylinder, rolling it gently inside the plastic wrap to form a symmetrical shape. (Alternatively, use a small ring mold to create cheese rounds.) Serve the cheese as is, or continue to customize it with one of the incredible variations that follow.

The cheese will last for up to 2 weeks and continue to firm up slightly in the refrigerator. It will also become slightly sharper with age. Alternatively, wrap the cheese tightly in plastic wrap, and then in aluminum foil, and store in the freezer for up to 6 months. Before serving, defrost the cheese for a couple of hours.

SUPERFOOD TIP: This cheese is very soft, like a goat cheese, when it is fresh. To further improve the texture, tightly wrap the cheese, after it has been molded into a round or ring. Freeze, then defrost, the cheese, a process that will make it slightly firmer and more fluffy. Alternatively, you can also place the cheese in a dehydrator—or oven, set at its lowest temperature—for a couple of hours to create a light rind on the exterior.

HEMP SEED CHEESE

I really like this very slight variation on Basic Superfood Cheese. The little chewy bits of hemp seeds in this recipe are both pleasant to eat and pretty to look at.

MAKES 4 ROUNDS / 16 SERVINGS

- 1 recipe Basic Superfood Cheese (page 100)
- ¼ cup hemp seeds

Place one-fourth of the cheese on a piece of plastic wrap. Shape the cheese into a 4-inch compact log and roll it gently inside the plastic wrap to form an even, symmetrical shape. Sprinkle the top with 1 tablespoon hemp seeds, and roll the log around in the seeds to coat the exterior surface. Repeat with remaining cheese to form 4 finished logs. (Alternatively, use a small ring mold to create cheese rounds, and press hemp seeds onto the top surface before removing the cheese from the mold.) To store, wrap tightly in plastic wrap and keep refrigerated for up to 2 weeks, or frozen for up to 2 months.

Serving suggestions: *Use Hemp Seed Cheese as a spread for crackers, flatbread, endive spears, thinly sliced radish rounds or cauliflower, and fresh fruit such as figs or pears.*

FEEL-GOOD FACT: In addition to protein, hemp seeds are also a fantastic source of magnesium, a mineral that supports relaxation, blood sugar control, and bone health.

GOJI BASIL CHEESE

I loved my trip to Italy, far too long ago, for its animated people, colorful layered landscapes, and unforgettable cheeses. I am reminded of that brief but blissful trip by the full flavor and freshness of this unique goji-infused cheese. Perhaps it's the essence of Italian culinary culture that shines through here: simple and fresh ingredients, done right.

MAKES 4 ROUNDS / 16 SERVINGS

- 2 tablespoons dried goji berries
- 2 heaping tablespoons fresh basil leaves, minced
- 1 recipe Basic Superfood Cheese (page 100)

FEEL-GOOD FACT: Eating goji berries is revered as an excellent way to naturally promote visionary heatlth and protect the eyes against degeneration, which is in part thanks to the red berry's high levels of a carotenoid antioxidant called zeaxanthin.

Soak the goji berries in enough water to cover them by about an inch for 10 minutes to partially soften. Drain water away, then coarsely chop the berries. In a small bowl, mix together the goji berries and basil.

Place one-fourth of the cheese mixture on a piece of plastic wrap. Shape the cheese into a 4-inch compact log and roll it gently inside the plastic wrap to form an even, symmetrical shape.

Sprinkle the top with 1 tablespoon of the goji mixture and roll the log around to coat the whole exterior surface. Repeat with remaining cheese to form 4 finished logs. (Alternatively, use a small ring mold to create cheese rounds, and top with goji basil mixture. After removing the cheese from the mold, lightly press additional berries and herbs into the sides.) To store, wrap tightly in plastic wrap and keep refrigerated for up to 1 week. Do not freeze.

Serving suggestions: *Use Goji Basil Cheese as a spread for crackers, flatbread, endive spears, and zucchini rounds.*

MAQUI BERRY & BLACK PEPPER CHEESE

Cheese may be delicious, but it's rarely described as "gorgeous" . . . except that's exactly what it is in this recipe. Although maqui doesn't add a lot of flavor to this soft cheese, every smear creates eye-catching electric-purple swirls that make each bite magical. It's a fun snack to serve when you're aiming for some oohs and aahs.

MAKES 4 ROUNDS / 16 SERVINGS

1½ teaspoons maqui berry powder

½ teaspoon freshly ground black pepper

1 recipe Basic Superfood Cheese (page 100)

Fresh lemon zest

In a small spice bowl, mix together the maqui berry powder and black pepper.

Place a quarter of the cheese mixture on a piece of plastic wrap. Shape the cheese into a 4-inch compact log and roll it gently inside the plastic wrap to form an even, symmetrical shape.

Sprinkle the top with ¼ teaspoon of the powder mixture and roll the log around to coat the whole exterior surface. Repeat with remaining cheese to form 4 finished logs. When ready to serve, sprinkle lightly with lemon zest. (Alternatively, use a small ring mold to create cheese rounds and top with maqui mixture before removing from the mold. Lightly press the maqui berry powder into the surface, and grate a little fresh lemon zest on top just before serving.) To store, wrap tightly in plastic wrap and keep refrigerated for up to 2 weeks, or frozen for up to 2 months.

Serving suggestions: *Use Maqui Berry & Black Pepper Cheese as a spread for crackers, flatbread, endive spears, and fresh fruit such as apricots, peaches, apples, or pears.*

FEEL-GOOD FACT: Maqui berries promote better circulation in the body, which can help energize the body as well as stimulate the brain.

COCONUT LABNEH

Labneh is a soft, Lebanese yogurt cheese spread that's coveted for a good reason—it's seductively smooth and creamy, yet it's lower in calories and fat than most other cheeses. Using coconut yogurt won't produce quite the same cream-cheese density as a traditional dairy labneh, but never fear: It will create an exquisitely creamy, tangy spread that has its own gorgeous flavor . . . and, as a bonus, it's cholesterol free. While I've coupled this recipe with summery fare in my serving suggestions below, labneh also pairs beautifully with mint and pomegranate seeds in the winter. It is an incredibly versatile spread, and you can truly mix in all kinds of flavors—spices such as cumin, fresh herbs, nuts and seeds, or bits of fresh or dried fruit.

MAKES 8 OUNCES / 4 SERVINGS

16 ounces unsweetened coconut yogurt

½ teaspoon sea salt

1 teaspoon probiotic powder*

¼ cup dried white mulberries, for garnish

1 cup fresh figs, quartered

Yacon syrup, for garnish

*Simply open probiotic capsules and empty the powder into a small bowl— a teaspoon is usually equivalent to 6 to 8 capsules.

Cut a double layer of cheesecloth in a 12-inch square. Lay the cloth inside a colander and place the colander inside a larger bowl, where the slowly strained liquid can collect.

In a medium bowl, whisk together the yogurt, sea salt, and probiotic powder until well combined. Spoon the yogurt into the center of the cheesecloth. Place inside a colander and over a bowl to catch excess liquid. Gather together the ends of the cloth and twist the excess fabric to form a ball of yogurt at the bottom, and loosely twist the excess fabric into a spiral on top. Do not squeeze the yogurt, or else it will push through the fabric. Refrigerate labneh for 2 to 3 days (longer refrigeration produces a slightly firmer spread).

Remove the cultured labneh from the refrigerator. Transfer it to a mixing bowl, inverting the fabric and squeezing out any mixture that remains on the cloth. Adjust the seasoning as desired and transfer to a serving bowl. When ready to serve, sprinkle with mulberries, fresh figs, and a drizzle of yacon syrup. Store in the refrigerator, covered tightly. Though the dip will continue to sharpen in flavor with time, it will last for several weeks without a garnish.

Serving suggestions: *Spread Coconut Labneh onto flatbreads and toasts (which can also be topped with roasted vegetables, sautéed greens, olives, or tomatoes). Or use as a dip for vegetables such as cucumbers and carrots, or fruits such as figs, peaches, or pears. Labneh makes just about any snack a special one!*

WHY COCONUT YOGURT?

Aren't we lucky to live at this time of yogurt opportunity! With varieties ranging from soy yogurt to Greek yogurt, almond milk yogurt to cow's milk yogurt, there are indeed oh-so-many options on the shelf. My favorite yogurt for the superfood kitchen is coconut yogurt, made from coconut milk. A third of the world's population is sensitive to dairy, and the number of people allergic to soy is rising too. Coconut yogurt is free from these common allergens, and is also much better for the body's pH balance. In terms of taste and texture, coconut yogurt is phenomenally rich (it doesn't taste like coconut, it just tastes creamy). Unlike almond milk yogurt or some other varieties which can be on the thinner side, coconut yogurt has a beautifully thick viscosity that feels absolutely divine, without being overly high in fat or calories. It's difficult to fully replicate store-bought coconut yogurt via a homemade recipe, so I recommend simply buying it at your local health food store, or even online (see page 209 for online resources). It goes without saying, you can swap coconut yogurt with another yogurt variety in a one-to-one ratio if you prefer, but if you haven't tried it, give this wonderful delicacy a try!

SAGE & HEMP SEED PESTO

Earthy yet bright, this sophisticated spread is delicious on just about anything, but for an incredible snack or appetizer, serve with Mochi Pesto Puffs (opposite)—they're mildly life-changing.

MAKES ABOUT ¾ CUP / 12 SERVINGS

¼ cup coconut oil

¼ cup fresh sage leaves

1 packed cup baby spinach

1 garlic clove, crushed

½ teaspoon sea salt

1 teaspoon yellow miso paste

2 tablespoons hemp seed oil or olive oil

½ teaspoon fresh lemon zest

1 teaspoon wheatgrass powder (optional)

½ cup hemp seeds

In a small skillet, melt the coconut oil over medium heat until very hot and simmering. Add the sage leaves and fry for about 3 minutes, stirring occasionally, until leaves are crisp. Remove the leaves from the pan with a slotted spoon and place them on a paper towel to cool. Pour the sage oil from the pan into a food processor or small blender.

Once the sage leaves are cool to the touch, add them to the food processor along with the spinach, garlic, salt, miso, hemp seed oil, lemon zest, and wheatgrass powder, if using. Process into a green paste, stopping the machine from time to time to scrape down the sides as needed. Add the hemp seeds and process once more to partially blend the seeds. Transfer the mixture to a bowl and serve warm or at room temperature. Pesto will thicken as it cools and become more of a spread, but it will easily melt if gently warmed. Store pesto in the refrigerator in a sealed container for up to 5 days, or freeze it in a covered ice cube tray for several months and melt down a cube whenever it's needed.

Serving suggestions: *Use Sage & Hemp Seed Pesto as a dip for vegetables, such as broccoli florets or carrots; as a spread on toast, crackers, sprouted-grain bread, or tortillas; or use it to make Mochi Pesto Puffs (page 109).*

FEEL-GOOD FACT: If you sweat excessively during exercise and hot weather, try adding a little sage to your diet. Sage is an anhidrotic, which helps prevent perspiration.

MOCHI PESTO PUFFS

These "puffs" are funny to look at, because the mochi has a tendency to form abstract shapes while it's cooking, but they're little bites of heaven served warm out of the oven, and they make an incredible snack or party appetizer. If you're not familiar with mochi, see page 209 for more information.

MAKES ABOUT 15 BITE-SIZE PUFFS / 5 SERVINGS

½ recipe Sage & Hemp Seed Pesto (page 108)

½ 12.5-ounce package mochi

Hemp seeds, for garnish (optional)

Preheat the oven to 450°F. Line a baking sheet with a silicone mat or parchment paper.

Cut the mochi into 1-inch squares. Place them on the prepared baking sheet, 2 inches apart, and bake for 10 to 12 minutes or until they puff up and begin to brown slightly. Remove the mochi puffs from the oven and let them rest for 1 to 2 minutes, until they're cool enough to handle, but still warm. Slice open the top of a puff to expose the hollow center and spoon in a little pesto spread. Repeat with the remaining puffs. If desired, sprinkle tops lightly with hemp seeds and top with a basil leaf. Serve immediately.

CHOCOLATE WHIP DIP

Whoever first discovered whipping chocolate and avocado together into a rich pudding-like dip deserves an award—it's pretty genius, and I haven't met a person yet who hasn't been floored by the simple and ultra-quick technique, not to mention the blissful results. My version is light but rich and chocolaty with just a hint of berry. And although it is superfood charged and sugar reduced, Chocolate Whip Dip is utterly (oh so utterly!) decadent. Serve it with fresh fruit as a dip (my favorite is chopped fresh mangos), or perhaps keep it on hand for the occasional, or not so occasional, delicious on-the-sly finger swipe.

MAKES APPROXIMATELY 2 CUPS / 8 SERVINGS

2 large soft avocados, peeled and pits removed

¼ cup unsweetened almond milk

¼ cup maple syrup

2 tablespoons agave syrup

10 drops liquid stevia extract

Pinch sea salt

6 tablespoons cacao powder

2 tablespoons acai berry powder

¼ teaspoon almond extract (optional)

Fresh fruit, for dipping (such as mangos, bananas, strawberries, and pineapple)

In a food processor, combine all the ingredients except the fresh fruit for dipping. Mix until a smooth puree has formed—you may have to stop the machine a few times to scrape down the sides. The key to this recipe is really making sure there are no avocado clumps, so keep processing until a silky-smooth, whipped consistency has been achieved—this may take a few minutes.

Transfer the chocolate whip to a bowl and serve with fresh fruit, if desired, for dipping.

SUPERFOOD BOOST: Add ¾ teaspoon spirulina powder for a secret serving of detoxifying greens—no one will ever know it's there!

HERBED CHICKPEA & YOGURT DIP

Think of this dip as a light (and low-calorie) hummus, whipped with generous amount of fresh herbs, while offering an invigorating tang. You can adjust its intensity by adding more or fewer herbs.

MAKES ABOUT 2 CUPS / 8 SERVINGS

1 14-ounce can unsalted chickpeas, rinsed and drained

½ cup unsweetened coconut yogurt

1 tablespoon tahini

¼ cup fresh lemon juice

1 teaspoon Dijon mustard

½ teaspoon sea salt

1 cup chopped parsley, plus sprigs for garnish

½ cup chopped mixed fresh herbs (such as dill, mint, tarragon, etc.), plus sprigs for garnish

2 green onions, white and green parts sliced thin

Olive oil, for garnish (optional)

Set aside a small handful of chickpeas for the garnish. Pour the remainder of the chickpeas into a food processor and add the yogurt, tahini, lemon juice, mustard, and sea salt. Process until smooth. Add the parsley, mixed herbs, and green onions, and pulse the machine a few times to incorporate. Transfer the mixture to a serving dish and garnish with reserved chickpeas, extra herb sprigs, and a drizzle of olive oil. Serve immediately. Stored in a covered container and refrigerated, the dip will last several days.

Serving suggestions: *Use Herbed Chickpea & Yogurt Dip to accompany carrots or sliced cucumbers, as a spread on toast or sprouted-grain bread, or brown rice crackers.*

Variation: *In place of the parsley, use fresh purslane, an incredible superfood vegetable that offers a lemony flavor and is an excellent source of omega-3's.*

MAKING HOMEMADE NUT BUTTERS

Once you break the ice and start making nut butters at home, the possibilities of using all kinds of nuts, seeds, and even superfood additions become tantalizingly endless. There are two ways to create these homemade spreads. One way is to use a food processor, which usually takes about 15 minutes to process a batch perfectly smooth. Food processors are an attractive option as they allow for extremely easy extraction of your freshly made butter. Alternatively, you can also use a high-speed blender. Simply combine the nut butter ingredients in the blender pitcher, and whiz on a low-medium speed for a full minute, or until the nuts are very smooth. Increase the speed to high to get an extra-smooth butter. (You may need to stop the blender to scrape down the sides before continuing to process the nuts.) Though initially faster, this method requires a little patience in removing the sticky nut butter from the crevices around the blender blades. Whichever method you choose, enjoy the cost-saving benefits—and fresh-made flavors—of making your own nut butters!

COCONUT BUTTER

Coconut butter—the happy, oh-so-happy marriage of coconut oil and coconut pulp—may not be a superfood in itself, but it is quite the indulgent natural ingredient to have in the pantry. Note that it is easy to buy this item pre-made in many natural food stores if you find yourself in a hurry!

MAKES 1½ CUPS / 24 SERVINGS

4½ cups dried shredded coconut (unsweetened)

2 tablespoons coconut oil (optional)

Place the coconut shreds in a food processor. Process for 2 to 3 minutes, then stop the machine and scrape down the sides. Continue to process for about 10 to 15 minutes, until coconut has liquefied (it will appear sandy for quite some time, but begin to transition to a liquid after about 10 minutes). At this point, you can add a little coconut oil, if desired, for a more spreadable butter, or leave as is. Transfer to a mason jar or container with a lid. Coconut butter can be refrigerated or stored at room temperature—it will harden when it is cool. To soften coconut butter, place it in a warm oven for 1 to 2 minutes or in a hot-water bath.

MACA CASHEW BUTTER

Think homemade honey peanut butter, and then imagine an even more addicting (and beneficial) version! You really get to experience maca's earthy-sweet, alluring flavor in full force in this recipe.

MAKES 1¼ CUPS / 10 SERVINGS

2 cups raw cashews

1½ tablespoons maca powder

¾ teaspoon ground cinnamon

½ teaspoon sea salt

3 tablespoons grapeseed oil

3 tablespoons maple syrup

½ teaspoon vanilla extract

Place the cashews, maca, cinnamon, and sea salt into the bowl of a food processor and grind into a flour—about 30 seconds. Add the grapeseed oil, maple syrup, and vanilla extract, and blend until a smooth, spreadable mixture has formed—about 10 to 12 minutes—stopping the machine and scraping down the sides as needed. Store Maca Cashew Butter in a lidded glass jar in the refrigerator, and it will last for several months.

Serving suggestions: *Spread this delicious butter on sprouted-grain bread; enjoy it with a banana or sliced pear; pack it inside a soft date; or just grab a spoon.*

Variation: *Try adding warm spices, such as cloves or nutmeg, to Maca Cashew Butter. You can also use yacon syrup in place of maple syrup, for a low glycemic option.*

POWER SEED BUTTER

This is what we call eating the spectrum! Why stop at just plain ol' almond butter when you can have protein-packed hemp, chia, and pumpkin seeds (pepitas) all at the same time? Deeply rich in minerals such as iron and healthy omega fats, this spread quickly transforms even a regular PB and J into an exciting superfood sandwich. In case you're wondering, the roasted almonds offer a little more flavor in this particular mixture, but you can certainly use raw as well . . . in fact, you can substitute all kinds of nuts and seeds to create your own variations.

MAKES 1½ CUPS / 12 SERVINGS

1 cup roasted unsalted almonds

½ cup hemp seeds

⅔ cup pepitas

1 tablespoon chia seeds

¼ teaspoon sea salt

2 tablespoons grapeseed oil

Put the almonds into the bowl of a food processor and grind them into a flour, about 30 seconds. Add the remaining ingredients and blend about 10 to 12 minutes, stopping the machine and scraping down the sides as needed. This will transform the mixture into a very smooth, creamy blend with a nice sheen. (It may take an extra couple of minutes to get the mixture smooth enough. Just continue processing until the nut butter is loose and spreadable.) Store Power Seed Butter in a glass jar with a lid in the refrigerator, and it will last for several months.

FEEL-GOOD FACT: Neuropathic doctors have discovered that pepitas have properties that can help treat prostate conditions effectively. Pepitas have high levels of fatty acids, zinc, and phytosterols, all of which support a healthy prostate.

ENERGY BARS & BITES

Not all bars are created equal. While some pre-packaged varieties can be classified as borderline glorified candy bars, homemade versions enable the use of nature's finest energy ingredients, and nothing more! Dried fruits, nuts, seeds and superfood powders come together to revolutionize the way we grab a quick bite: from exotic Goldenberry Pistachio Bars to homey Cookie Dough Protein Bites made with real cacao. The world of energy bars is flexible and vast, and one of the quickest homemade snacks to make for on-the-go lifestyles.

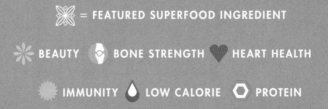

= FEATURED SUPERFOOD INGREDIENT

BEAUTY   BONE STRENGTH   HEART HEALTH

IMMUNITY   LOW CALORIE   PROTEIN

(SUPERFOOD) KITCHEN SINK ENERGY BALLS

Here it is: "The ball that started it all." If you've read any of my personal story in Superfood Kitchen *you may remember how I came to work with superfoods. I talk about getting my first bag of goji berries and maca root in college . . . and having no idea what do with them. So, I made "balls." They may have needed a little tweaking in the flavor department, but they sure worked in terms of providing energy, and I've been lovingly refining them ever since. I now call this my "kitchen sink" recipe because it's so highly adaptable: It's a giant YES to substituting, adding, or leaving out almost any superfood you have on hand.*

MAKES 1½ DOZEN / 9 SERVINGS

⅓ cup Medjool dates (about 5–6 large), pitted

½ cup walnuts

½ cup dried shredded coconut (unsweetened)

2 tablespoons maca powder

1 tablespoon chia seeds

1 tablespoon hemp seeds

⅛ teaspoon sea salt

¼ cup dried goji berries

In a food processor, mix together the dates, walnuts, coconut, maca powder, chia seeds, hemp seeds, and sea salt. Process until a moist, crumb-like dough has formed. Stop the machine and check the consistency: Depending on the natural moisture of the dates, you may need to add a touch of water—1 teaspoon at a time—to get the crumbs to stick together when pinched. Once the proper consistency has been achieved, add the goji berries and pulse to incorporate and coarsely chop the goji berries into the blend, leaving a bit of texture.

Scoop a tablespoon of the dough into your hands, and squeeze and roll it into a compact ball. Repeat using the remainder of the dough.

Energy balls will last several weeks unrefrigerated and covered, or keep them in the freezer for long-term storage.

SUPERFOOD BOOST: Don't be shy about throwing in a spoonful of your favorite superfood powders, such as maqui berry, camu berry, or spirulina. Just be sure to taste as you go!

CHOCOLATE CHERRY GOJI BARS

Cherries and goji berries are soulmates in the dried-fruit world—I often make trail mixes that pair these two red beauties. Here, they're friends again in these wholesome, cacao-nib-accented raw bars. Packed with all kinds of antioxidants, these bars appear to be "only" sweet treats, while undercover they are anti-aging workhorses.

MAKES 8 BARS / 8 SERVINGS

½ cups raw walnuts

¾ cup raw almonds

¼ cup Medjool dates (about 3–4 large), pitted

½ cup dried goji berries

1 teaspoon vanilla extract

⅛ teaspoon ground cinnamon

1 cup dried cherries

2 tablespoons cacao nibs

In a food processor, combine the walnuts and the almonds, and process the nuts into the size of small gravel. Add the dates, goji berries, vanilla extract, and cinnamon powder, and process until the mixture forms clumps and begins to stick together. Add the cherries and cacao nibs and process briefly to incorporate the ingredients, but leave some small chunks for texture. Stop the machine and check the consistency: Depending on the natural moisture of the dates, you may need to add a touch of water—1 teaspoon at a time—to get the crumbs to stick together when pinched. If the dough is too wet, blend in a few extra almonds.

Place the dough on a large sheet of plastic wrap on a cutting board. Press the dough into a compact rectangle, then wrap it tightly in the plastic, compacting it even more. Use a rolling pin to roll the dough into a ½-inch-thick layer. Unwrap the dough and cut it into bars or bites as desired. Energy bars will last several weeks unrefrigerated and covered, or keep them in the freezer for long-term storage.

SUPERFOOD BOOST: Add ½ teaspoon spirulina powder while blending the ingredients for a mineral-rich green upgrade.

MOCHA ENERGY BITES

You'll find big flavor and big-time energy here. If you're avoiding caffeine, simply use decaffeinated instant coffee granules instead of regular coffee in these bites.

MAKES 24 BITES / 8 SERVINGS

1 cup raw hazelnuts

1 teaspoon instant coffee granules

2 tablespoons vanilla protein powder

Pinch sea salt

⅔ cup Medjool dates (about 11–12), pitted

3 tablespoons cacao nibs

2 tablespoons chia seeds

Place the hazelnuts, coffee granules, protein powder, and sea salt in a food processor and grind into a coarse flour. Add the dates and process into a "dough." Add the cacao nibs and chia seeds, and process once more very briefly, leaving a little bit of texture. Stop the machine and check the consistency: Depending on the natural moisture of the dates, you may need to add a touch of water—½ teaspoon at a time—to get the crumbs to stick together when pinched. If the dough is too wet, mix in a little extra protein powder.

Place the dough on a large sheet of plastic wrap on a cutting board. Press the dough into a compact square, then tightly wrap it in the plastic to further compress the dough into a 1-inch-thick slab. Unwrap and cut the dough into 24 small rounded squares. Alternately, simply use your hands to form the dough into bites.

Bites may be stored at room temperature in an airtight container for several weeks, or in the freezer for several months.

SUPERFOOD BOOST: Add 1 teaspoon wheatgrass powder for a stealthy upgrade of detoxifying (and also energizing!) greens.

GREEN BANANA–COCONUT CRUNCH BITES

I have a love-hate relationship with banana chips: I hate that I love to eat them uncontrollably, as if I'm Ms. Pac-Man. These bites, on the other hand, satisfy my craving for crunch really nicely, while also giving me all the energizing benefits of spirulina (which you can see, but can't taste) and feel-good hemp seeds.

MAKES 24 BITES / 8 SERVINGS

1⅓ cups unsweetened banana chips, divided

½ cup Medjool dates (about 7–8 large), pitted

¾ teaspoon spirulina powder

1 teaspoon vanilla extract

Pinch sea salt

¼ cup shredded unsweetened coconut

3 tablespoons hemp seeds

Place 1 cup of the banana chips in a food processor and grind into gravel-sized bits. Add the dates, spirulina powder, vanilla extract, and sea salt, and process into a chunky "dough." Stop the machine and check the consistency: Depending on the natural moisture of the dates, you may need to add a touch of water—½ teaspoon at a time—to get the crumbs to stick together when pinched. If the dough is too wet, mix in a little extra coconut in the next step, 1 tablespoon at a time.

Add the coconut shreds and hemp seeds, and process to distribute. Add the remaining ⅓ cup banana chips and process for several seconds to just break them apart, but leave in some crunchy bits.

Place the dough on top of a large sheet of plastic wrap on a cutting board. Press the dough into a compact square. Then tightly wrap it in the plastic, compacting the dough even more into a 6-inch square. Unwrap the dough and cut it into 24 small squares. Alternately, simply use your hands to form the dough into rounded bites.

Green Banana–Coconut Crunch Bites may be stored at room temperature in an airtight container for several weeks, or in the freezer for several months.

Note: *If you can't find unsweetened banana chips, choose a variety with the lowest sugar possible.*

GOLDENBERRY PISTACHIO BARS

In this recipe, goldenberries sing their sweet-and-tart song loud and proud. These delightful bars are a little citrusy, a little nutty, and far from the norm.

MAKES 8 BARS / 8 SERVINGS

⅔ cup Medjool dates (about 6–7 large), pitted

⅔ cup raw almonds

2 tablespoons chia seeds

1 teaspoon freshly squeezed lemon juice, or more as needed

⅔ cup unsalted shelled pistachios

⅔ cup dried goldenberries

In a food processor, combine the dates, almonds, chia seeds and lemon juice, and process into a thick dough. Add the pistachios and goldenberries, and process until the mixture sticks together but is still chunky. If the dough is too dry, add a little more lemon juice—1 teaspoon at a time—until it sticks easily when pressed between two fingers.

Place the dough on a large sheet of plastic wrap on a cutting board. Press the dough into a compact square. Then tightly wrap it in the plastic, compacting it even further into a 6-inch square. Unwrap the dough and cut into bars or bites as desired. Energy bars will last several weeks unrefrigerated and covered, or keep them in the freezer for long-term storage.

Variation: *For an unusual flavor upgrade, add a few pinches of finely minced fresh rosemary when you blend the dates and almonds.*

APRICOT ACAI BITES

At first glance, these may look like typical energy bites, but after one taste you'll appreciate the difference, as layers of spiced-fruit flavor excitingly unfold in your mouth. Although it may seem picky, be sure to use Turkish dried apricots—they are so deliciously plump and sweet, in comparison to other dried-out, leathery varieties. If you can't find them, use the best sulfite-free dried apricots you can get your hands on, and add some raisins to the mixture to improve the texture and taste, as needed.

MAKES 24 BITES / 8 SERVINGS

½ cup raw almonds

¾ cup unsulfured dried Turkish apricots

¼ cup acai berry powder

2 tablespoons hemp seeds

¼ teaspoon ginger powder

¼ teaspoon ground black pepper

⅛ teaspoon sea salt

½ teaspoon vanilla extract

1 tablespoon agave nectar

Add all the ingredients to a food processor and grind into a coarse dough, leaving a bit of texture. Stop the machine and check the consistency: Depending on the natural moisture of the dates, you may need to add a touch of water—½ teaspoon at a time—to get the crumbs to stick together when pinched together. If the dough is too wet, mix in a few more almonds.

Place the dough on a large sheet of plastic wrap on a cutting board. Press the dough into a compact square, then tightly wrap it in the plastic to further compress the dough into a 1-inch-thick slab. Cut the dough into 24 small squares. Alternately, simply use your hands to form the dough into bites.

Apricot Acai Bites may be stored at room temperature in an airtight container for several weeks, or in the freezer for several months.

Variation: *If you're a mega ginger lover and want bigger, bolder flavor, skip the agave and add a few spoonfuls of candied ginger when you add the almonds and apricots.*

ARABIAN AMARANTH BALLS

Oh, those Arabic spices—they get me every time! Deeply aromatic and bursting with exotic flavors, these unusual snacks are a wonderful diversion from the average ho-hum fruit-and-nut ball. With their sweet-savory balance, these amaranth balls are incredibly enchanting. If, by chance, you happen to have sumac powder in your spice cabinet (it's one of the highest antioxidant spices in the world!), this recipe would be a wonderful place to use it.

MAKES 30 BALLS / 15 SERVINGS

1 cup raw pistachios

1 teaspoon wheatgrass powder

1½ teaspoons turmeric powder

½ teaspoon cumin powder

½ teaspoon curry powder

½ teaspoon sea salt

½ cup raw sunflower seeds

¼ cup Medjool dates (about 3–4 large), pitted

2 tablespoons almond butter

2 tablespoons fresh lemon juice

¼ cup golden raisins

⅔ cup Popped Amaranth (page 71), divided

In a food processor, combine the pistachios, wheatgrass, turmeric, cumin, curry, and sea salt. Process to grind the nuts into a coarse gravel. Add the sunflower seeds, dates, almond butter and lemon juice, and mix until a sticky "dough" has formed. Add the raisins and ⅓ cup of the popped amaranth, and pulse the machine a few times—just enough to incorporate, but leaving plenty of texture. Transfer the mixture to a bowl. Pour the remaining ⅓ cup popped amaranth into a small bowl.

Form the dough, one rounded teaspoon at a time, into compact balls, and roll them in the remaining popped amaranth to coat the exterior. Repeat with the remaining dough. Balls can be stored at room temperature or refrigerated for up to 1 week in a sealed container, or can be frozen for several weeks.

FEEL-GOOD FACT: Think twice about that bottle of Ibuprofen and consider turmeric instead for natural pain relief. Turmeric has been used in traditional medicine to ease the pain of sprains, strains, bruises and joint inflammation very effectively! The healing power of turmeric comes from its active ingredient—curcumin, which lowers the levels of bodily enzymes that cause inflammation.

STUFFED DATES

When it comes to sweet snacking, I wholly admit to a mild obsession with dates! Sure, they're a go-to ingredient as a smart sugar substitute in healthy dessert making, yet fresh, soft dates are also exquisitely delicious eaten by themselves . . . or, even better, split open and stuffed with treatworthy fillings for a simple bite of sheer bliss. Stuffed dates are a great way to pack in many superfoods all at once, supplying a rainbow of quick, portable, high-energy natural snacking—a game-changing, healthy shortcut for on-the-go lifestyles.

Here are some especially good, simple date "stuffings" to try, with or without superfood ingredients:

- ◆ Nuts—higher-fat nuts such as walnuts, pecans, and macadamia nuts
- ◆ Seeds—especially higher-fat seeds, such as hemp seeds and sacha inchi seeds
- ◆ Nut/seed butters—almond butter and coconut butter are exceptional
- ◆ Cacao nibs—while processed chocolate is too sweet for dates, deep, dark cacao nibs offer a seductively bitter contrast
- ◆ Unsweetened coconut shreds—dates and coconut are best friends
- ◆ Solidified coconut oil—use up to 1 teaspoon per date for a pure energy snack. (One or two of these makes an exceptional pre-workout food choice.)

COOKIE DOUGH PROTEIN BITES

The fact that almost half of the ingredients in these bites are considered the best-of-the-best superfoods should be the first clue that this snack is not messing around, despite its disguise as a craveable cookie-dough-flavored treat.

MAKES 24 BITES / 12 SERVINGS

1 cup dried white mulberries

⅓ cup Medjool dates (about 5–6), pitted

⅓ cup almond butter

⅓ cup vanilla protein powder

1 teaspoon vanilla extract

⅛ teaspoon sea salt

¼ cup dried goji berries

¼ cup hemp seeds

¼ cup semi-sweet mini chocolate chips

SUPERFOOD BOOST: Add 2 tablespoons cacao nibs in addition to, or instead of, the chocolate chips.

In a food processor, grind the mulberries into a coarse mixture. Add the dates, almond butter, protein powder, vanilla extract, and sea salt, and process until well combined. Stop the machine, then add the goji berries, hemp seeds, and chocolate chips. Briefly process once more to break down the ingredients, while allowing some large pieces to remain for texture. Stop the machine and check the consistency: Depending on the natural moisture of the dates, you may need to add a touch of water—1 teaspoon at a time—to get the crumbs to stick together when pinched together. If the dough is too wet, mix in a little extra protein powder.

For a cookie-dough-like effect, take a small melon ball scoop and fill it to the top with dough, packing it in tightly with your fingers, then release the circular scoop of dough. Repeat with remaining dough.

Alternatively, place the dough on a large sheet of plastic wrap on a cutting board. Press the dough into a compact square, then tightly wrap it in the plastic to further compress the dough into a 1-inch-thick slab. Cut the dough into 24 small squares.

Cookie Dough Protein Bites may be stored at room temperature in an airtight container for several weeks, or in the freezer for several months.

PROTEIN-PACKED STUFFED DATES

These grab-and-go treats, with their balance of high-quality protein, healthy fats, quick carbohydrates, and essential fiber are a powerhouse of yum.

MAKES 24 BITES / 12 SERVINGS

18 large Medjool dates

⅓ cup creamy almond butter (unsalted)

3 tablespoons pure hemp protein powder

1 tablespoon coconut oil

2 teaspoons vanilla extract

½ teaspoon almond extract

⅛ teaspoon sea salt

¼ cup dried goji berries

¼ cup raw walnuts

½ cup hemp seeds

¼ cup superfood seeds (hemp seeds, chia seeds, flaxseeds) for rolling

To prepare the dates, use a small paring knife to make a clean incision lengthwise down one side of each date, and carefully remove the pit to create a "canoe."

Place 4 of the dates in a food processor, and add the almond butter, hemp protein powder, coconut oil, vanilla extract, almond extract, and sea salt. Process until a thick paste has formed. Add the goji berries, walnuts and hemp seeds, and blend for a moment to chop the ingredients, while allowing some texture to remain.

Place ¼ cup of the superfood seeds into a small bowl.

Spoon about 1 tablespoon of the filling inside the cavity (or "canoe") of each date, using your fingers to press and tightly pack in the mixture. Then press the filled side of each date into the superfood seeds to coat the surface. Serve at room temperature or refrigerated.

Note: *These stuffed dates will keep for several weeks in the fridge, and may also be frozen for long-term storage up to several months. Be sure to wrap them well.*

ACAI-MINT STUFFED DATES

This is a dream date . . . and I'm not just going for a cheap pun either. I actually had a dream about foraging, and "came across" this combination of acai berry and mint. Upon waking, I gave it a try, and couldn't help but give my subconscious a sincere tip of the hat. Because these dates use fresh mint, they last only a couple of days. If you don't think you'll go through them quickly, simply prepare the recipe without the mint and add it later, when you're ready to enjoy these treats in all their glory.

MAKES 12 SNACKS / 12 SERVINGS

12 large Medjool dates

2 tablespoons cacao nibs (optional)

3 tablespoons acai berry powder

⅓ cup coconut butter (page 114)

2 tablespoons maple syrup

¼ cup mint leaves, minced

To prepare the dates, use a small paring knife to make a clean incision lengthwise down one side of each date, and carefully remove the pit to create a "canoe." Place the cacao nibs in a small bowl or dish and set aside.

In a small bowl, use a fork to mash and mix together the acai berry powder, coconut butter, and maple syrup. Depending on the kind you use, the coconut butter may remain a little chunky—this is perfectly okay (it can provide a nice texture).

Press a pinch of fresh mint into the bottom of each date, just as you would fill a taco. Using your hands, roll the acai filling, 1 teaspoon at a time, into a small ball, and then form it into a log. Press the filling into the cavity of the date, and then press the date, filling side down, into the dish of cacao nibs for garnish.

FEEL-GOOD FACT: One of the many reasons acai is such a popular power food is its exceptionally high antioxidants: it contains 10 times more than grapes, and up to twice that of blueberries.

CHEF'S CHOICE GRANOLA BARS

Granola bars have a real carpe diem vibe about them: once you have a solid base (like the recipe here), you, the baker, can get away with adding in all kinds of goodies to give them your own signature flair. From dried cherries to mulberries to hemp seeds, the world of accouterments is a flexible one. One of my favorite "choices" with this recipe is equal parts of freshly-toasted crushed hazelnuts, cacao nibs, and goji berries.

MAKES 10 BARS

1½ cups rolled oats*

¼ cup coconut sugar

2 teaspoons maca powder

½ teaspoon sea salt

1 teaspoon ground cinnamon

½ cup salted roasted almonds, chopped fine

¼ cup chia seeds

¼ cup flaxseeds

½ cup your choice chopped nuts, dried fruit, or superfoods

2 tablespoons coconut oil

¼ cup smooth almond butter

¼ cup maple syrup

*Gluten-free rolled oats may be used.

Line an 8 x 8-inch pan with parchment paper, allowing the paper to spill over the sides for easy removal.

In a medium bowl, mix together the oats, coconut sugar, maca powder, sea salt, cinnamon, almonds, chia seeds, flaxseeds, and superfood add-ins of your choice.

In a large skillet, heat the coconut oil over medium high heat. Stir in the almond butter. Add in the dry ingredients, mixing to incorporate and warm the ingredients, about 1 to 2 minutes. Pour in the maple syrup, stirring constantly, until all excess liquid has evaporated, about 1 minute. Transfer the contents to the prepared pan, and spread out evenly. Use the back of a spatula to press firmly into an even, flat layer. Refrigerate for one hour to solidify, then cut into 10 bars. Bars can be stored refrigerated or at room temperature (they will remain more firm if refrigerated). Stored in a sealed container, they will keep for up to 1 week.

CANDIES & CHOCOLATE

Indulge with pride. Sweet, rich, and sometimes downright naughty-tasting, superfood candies such as truffles and fudge satisfy sugar cravings while offering invigorating benefits. Antioxidant leader cacao plays a huge role in making show-stopping chocolates, while other featured superfoods include goji berries, mulberries, acai and maqui. With first-rate superfoods like these in tow, there's no excuse not to treat yourself anytime you wish!

 = FEATURED SUPERFOOD INGREDIENT

 BEAUTY   BONE STRENGTH   HEART HEALTH

 IMMUNITY   LOW CALORIE  PROTEIN

SALTED ALMOND CHOCOLATE BARK

Although Himalayan salt is used as an optional garnish in this recipe (it's slightly sweeter than other salts and can be cracked on the spot with a grinder), you can also experiment with other fun specialty salts, such as black lava salt or wood-smoked salt. Just remember to use a very light touch when garnishing the chocolate—at the end of the day, salt is still salt!

MAKES ABOUT 10 OUNCES (BY WEIGHT) / 8 SERVINGS

½ cup cacao butter, cut into shavings

¼ cup cacao powder

1 teaspoon spirulina powder

2 tablespoons agave nectar

⅓ cup dry-roasted salted almonds, chopped

2 tablespoons hemp seeds

Cracked Himalayan salt, or other specialty salt (optional)

Place a ceramic dinner plate in the freezer to chill.

Melt the cacao butter using a double boiler method: Heat a large pot of water to a near boil and turn off the heat. Put the cacao shavings into a metal bowl about the same size as the pot, and rest it on top of the water. Allow the shavings to slowly melt into a liquid. Take care not to get any water in the cacao butter.

Once the butter is melted, transfer the bowl to a countertop, and whisk in the cacao powder and spirulina powder until combined. Add the agave nectar and whisk briskly for about 30 seconds—the chocolate will begin to thicken as it cools, so work quickly. Add the almonds and hemp seeds and stir to incorporate. Remove the chilled plate from the freezer and pour the chocolate on top. Dust the top with Himalayan salt (very lightly), if desired. Return the plate to the freezer and chill for about 20 to 30 minutes, or until chocolate is completely solid. Use a mini spatula or dull knife to carefully pry up and snap off chunks of the chocolate. Larger pieces can be broken up further if desired. Chocolate bark will remain hard at room temperature. For long-term storage, keep the bark in the refrigerator, wrapped in foil, where it will keep for about 6 weeks.

MAPLE PECAN CHOCOLATE BARK

Not too sweet, the chocolate offers a beautiful maple note and a subtle crunch from the pecans and the sugar crystals, so every chew seems to melt away with flavor. A few of the ingredients may seem a little extravagant—such as the vanilla bean and maple sugar, which aren't used very much in other recipes in this book— but the results are so worth it.

MAKES 14 OUNCES (BY WEIGHT) / 10 SERVINGS

3 tablespoons raw pecans

⅛ teaspoon sea salt

1 vanilla bean, split, seeds scraped

5 tablespoons maple sugar

1 cup cacao butter, cut into small shavings

¾ cup + 2 tablespoons cacao powder

Place a ceramic dinner plate in the freezer to chill.

Heat a small sauté pan over medium-high heat. When hot, add the pecans and toast, stirring occasionally, until fragrant, 4 to 5 minutes. Let the pecans cool for a moment, then chop them into fine pieces and set aside.

Use a mortar and pestle to grind the salt, vanilla seeds, and maple sugar into a fine powder. The finer the powder, the better.

Melt the cacao butter using a double boiler method: Heat a large pot of water to a near boil and turn off the heat. Put the cacao shavings into a metal bowl about the same size as the pot, and rest it on top of the water. Allow the shavings to slowly melt into a liquid. Take care not to get any water in the cacao butter.

Once the butter is fully melted, remove the pot from the hot water bath and whisk in all the cacao powder until smooth. Add the sugar mixture and whisk very well. Remove the plate from the freezer and pour the liquid chocolate on top. Sprinkle the chocolate with pecans. Return the plate to the freezer for 20 to 30 minutes or until the chocolate is completely solid. Use a butter knife or other dull utensil to carefully pry up and snap off chunks of the chocolate. Break it into pieces. The chocolate will remain hard at room temperature, and will soften easily when exposed to heat. For long-term storage, keep the chocolate in the refrigerator, wrapped in foil, where it will keep for about 6 weeks.

CHOCOLATE CHILI TRUFFLES

Chocolate and spices have long been a popular combination in Central and South America, and continue to be a Mexican specialty. In truffle form, you can't help but swoon over the combo, which teases with just a little bit of heat.

MAKES 18 TRUFFLES / 9 SERVINGS

⅓ cup Medjool dates (about 5-6 large), pitted

¼ cup cacao butter, melted

2 tablespoons coconut oil

2 tablespoons agave nectar

2 tablespoons coconut sugar

½ cup cacao powder

1 teaspoon vanilla extract

⅛ teaspoon sea salt

1 tablespoon ground cinnamon

1 tablespoon chili powder

⅛ teaspoon cayenne powder

In a food processor, blend all the ingredients into a smooth mixture. You may have to stop the machine several times to scrape down the sides to ensure that all the ingredients are incorporated evenly. When the mixture has formed a large, smooth ball inside of the food processor, transfer it to a bowl, cover, and refrigerate for 30 minutes to partially solidify.

Once it is chilled and pliable, remove the truffle mixture from the refrigerator. Measuring 1 tablespoon at a time, form the dough into a smooth ball with your hands. Repeat with remaining dough.

Truffles are best served at room temperature (they will become more solid when refrigerated, and very soft in extreme heat). For long-term storage, keep the truffles in the refrigerator in an airtight container, where they will keep for about 6 weeks.

Note: *Be sure to check the ingredients of your chili powder to ensure it is 100 percent chili, and not a blend of savory ingredients.*

Variation: *Roll the truffles in a 1:1 mixture of cacao powder and lucuma for a light dusting of extra flavor.*

SALTED MACA TRUFFLES

This melt-in-your-mouth treat celebrates the beautiful, complex flavor of maca, which, when it is used in the right format (such as these truffles), can be an outstandingly special experience.

MAKES 14 TRUFFLES / 7 SERVINGS

¼ cup cashew butter, or almond butter (unsalted)

½ cup coconut butter

¼ cup coconut sugar

2 tablespoons maple syrup

¼ cup melted cacao butter

1 tablespoon maca powder

¼ teaspoon almond extract

¼ teaspoon sea salt

2 tablespoons lucuma powder, divided

Flaked sea salt

In a food processor, combine the cashew butter (or almond butter), coconut butter, coconut sugar, maple syrup, cacao butter, maca powder, almond extract, sea salt, and 1 tablespoon of the lucuma powder. Process until smooth. Transfer the contents to a bowl, cover, and refrigerate for 30 minutes to partially solidify.

Place the remaining 1 tablespoon lucuma powder in a small bowl. Pour a little flaked sea salt in another small bowl. Line a plate with parchment or wax paper.

Once chilled and pliable, remove the truffle mixture from the refrigerator. One tablespoon at a time, roll the mixture into a smooth ball. Roll the ball in the lucuma powder to dust the surface, and lightly dip just the top of the ball into the salt bowl to form a crown of salt. Gently tap the ball to remove any excess salt, and place on the lined plate. Repeat with the remaining mixture. Place the balls in the refrigerator to firm up for an additional 30 minutes before serving. These truffles are best when they are served chilled, and will last up to 1 week if they are covered and refrigerated.

Variation: *Spice up these truffles with 1 teaspoon of ground cinnamon and a pinch of cayenne pepper.*

MAQUI MINT TRUFFLES

Go ahead: It's okay to be a little smug about your new dessert addiction. For though these truffles taste like the most exquisite chocolate-mint divinity a candy shop might offer, a bounty of secret superfoods, offering anti-aging and detoxifcation benefits, is tucked away within each sweet bite.

MAKES 1 DOZEN / 6 SERVINGS

⅓ cup Medjool dates (about 5–6 large), pitted

6 tablespoons cacao powder

1½ tablespoons maqui berry powder

½ teaspoon spirulina or chlorella powder

¼ cup cacao butter, melted

2 tablespoons coconut oil

2 tablespoons agave nectar

¾ teaspoon mint extract

¼ teaspoon vanilla extract

Pinch sea salt

2 tablespoons cacao nibs

1 tablespoon coconut sugar

In a food processor, blend all the ingredients except for the cacao nibs and coconut sugar into a smooth mixture. You may have to stop the machine several times to scrape down the sides to ensure that all the ingredients are incorporated evenly. When the mixture has formed a large, smooth ball inside of the food processor, transfer it to a bowl, cover, and refrigerate for 30 minutes to partially solidify.

Meanwhile, use a spice grinder or blender to briefly grind the cacao nibs and coconut sugar together into a coarse powder. Place the mix in a small bowl and set it aside.

Once chilled and pliable, remove the truffle mixture from the refrigerator. Measuring 1 tablespoon at a time, form the dough into a smooth ball with your hands, then roll the ball in the cacao-nib powder to dust the exterior. Repeat with remaining dough.

Truffles are best served at room temperature (they will become more solid when refrigerated, and very soft in extreme heat). For long-term storage, keep the truffles in the refrigerator in an airtight container, where they will keep for about 6 weeks.

FEEL-GOOD FACT: One long term study found that a square of dark chocolate a day reduced the risk of heart attack and stroke by 39 percent. This is thanks to the flavonoid antioxidants in chocolate, which are found in even greater quantities in its original cacao form.

DARK CHOCOLATE ORANGE TRUFFLES

Big flavor sometimes comes in small (and sophisticated) packages. Despite their undeniable decadence, these unforgettable truffles also do away with guilt by using only the very best superfood ingredients, including antioxidant-rich raw cacao, sustainable coconut sugar and dates, and energy-giving coconut oil.

MAKES 20 TRUFFLES / 10 SERVINGS

⅔ cup cacao powder

⅔ cup Medjool dates (about 9–10 large), pitted

2 tablespoons orange zest, divided

2 tablespoons orange juice

¼ cup coconut oil

Pinch sea salt

3 tablespoons coconut sugar

Use a food processor to mix together all the ingredients except the coconut sugar and 1 tablespoon of the orange zest into a smooth dough. In a separate bowl, mix the coconut sugar and remaining orange zest to form an orange-flavored sugar.

To make the truffles, remove the "dough" from the processor and roll a small amount, about 1 tablespoon at a time, into a ball. Lightly press the top half of the ball into the sugar mixture and transfer it to a serving plate. Repeat the process to make the remaining truffles.

Cover and place the truffles in the freezer for a minimum of 30 minutes or until you are ready to enjoy them. Serve chilled. For long-term storage, keep the truffles in the refrigerator in an airtight container, where they will keep for about 6 weeks.

> **FEEL-GOOD FACT:** It may be a fat, but coconut oil is a heart-healthy friend, not a foe. Its saturated fats are in the form of medium-chain fatty acids (MCFA's) that actually boost good cholesterol, and it has also shown to lower the bad types of cholesterol in the body that lead to cardiovascular disease.

PEANUT BUTTER GINGER CANDY CHEWS

These chewy Tootsie Roll–size treats are a must-make for ginger lovers. Although you can make them with almond butter, they really do taste the best with peanut butter.

MAKES 24 ROLLS / 12 SERVINGS

½ cup + 2 tablespoons dried white mulberries, divided

2 tablespoons peanut butter

2 tablespoons coconut sugar

2 tablespoons lucuma powder, plus extra for dusting

1 tablespoon + 1 teaspoon grated peeled fresh ginger

½ teaspoon ginger powder

Place ½ cup of the dried mulberries in a food processor and blend for a full minute, or until the berries are ground very finely. Add the peanut butter, coconut sugar, lucuma powder, fresh ginger, and ginger powder, and process again until all ingredients are incorporated. Add the remaining 2 tablespoons mulberries and blend for a few seconds to break down the berries into coarse pieces.

Transfer the "dough" to a flat surface and divide it in half. Gather one of the halves into a ball. Knead and squeeze it for a moment to fully incorporate the ingredients and continue to compress the dough into a tightly packed ball. Form the ball into a sausage-like shape, place it on a flat surface, and roll it into a 12-inch rope with your hands. Use a sharp knife to cut the rope into 12 pieces, wiping off the knife with a moist cloth between cuts to make clean slices. Repeat the process with the second half of the mixture, and place the rolls to the side.

Lightly sprinkle lucuma powder over a palm-size flat surface. One at a time, roll the rolls in the lucuma powder, dusting off any extra powder. The rolls can be served at room temperature, but wrap and chill the rolls to store, to keep the fresh ginger from spoiling. The rolls will keep for 1 week in the refrigerator.

MULBERRY LICORICE CHEWS

I used to be a card-carrying member of the "black licorice is terrible" club, until one day I had GOOD black licorice, and my life was changed forever. This recipe, albeit an untraditional one in the world of licorice candy, is a great example of just how intensely flavorful pure, natural foods can be—but don't be fooled by its simplicity! Plus there's an extra bonus: fennel seeds, a known digestive aid and breath freshener, which make these chews a perfect after-dinner refreshment.

MAKES 2 DOZEN / 8 SERVINGS

3 tablespoons dried fennel seeds, divided

1½ cups dried white mulberries

1 tablespoon maqui berry powder

1 tablespoon agave nectar

Place 2 tablespoons of the fennel seeds in a spice grinder and process for several seconds into a very fine powder.

In a food processor, add the freshly ground fennel powder, mulberries, maqui berry powder, and agave, and blend until a sticky, coarse mixture has formed.

Spoon the remaining tablespoon of fennel seeds into a small bowl or dish. Use your fingers to form the mulberry mixture, one teaspoon at a time, into compact small rolls. Tap one side of each roll into the fennel seeds to decorate the top with a few seeds—you don't want too many—just enough to add an extra flavor punch. Serve the chews at room temperature, and store them covered in the refrigerator for up to several weeks.

> **SUPERFOOD TIP:** For a nostalgic presentation, wrap each roll in candy wrappers or parchment paper.

PEPPERMINT PATTIES

Disks of soft and sweet minty magic enveloped in dark chocolate . . . yes, please.

MAKES 24 PATTIES / 12 SERVINGS

1 cup dried shredded coconut (unsweetened)

¼ cup agave nectar

1½ teaspoons peppermint extract

6 drops liquid stevia

½ teaspoon spirulina powder

1 batch Basic Superfood Chocolate (page 150)

SUPERFOOD TIP: If you don't have a small cookie cutter on hand—use a bottle cap instead! Or, simply use a knife to slice the "dough" into 1½-inch squares.

In a food processor, combine the coconut, agave, mint extract, and liquid stevia. Process for several minutes, until the coconut has broken down and a coarse paste has formed. Add the spirulina and process to mix in. Stop the machine and form the mixture into a ball. Line a flat surface with a one foot-long piece of plastic wrap. Place the peppermint ball in the middle of the wrap, along with any excess oil that may have separated in the bowl, and cover the ball loosely with a second piece of plastic wrap. Use a rolling pin to flatten the ball into an even ¼-inch-thick slab. Use a 1½-inch diameter round cookie cutter to cut the dough into rounds. Place the rounds on a plate lined with parchment paper. pumpkin any excess dough, flatten it again, and form it into rounds to use up all of the dough. Cover it loosely, and freeze for 30 minutes.

Once the patties are chilled, melt the chocolate gently in a small saucepan over very low heat. When the chocolate is fully liquefied, remove it from the heat. Leave the chocolate in the warm pan—if it begins to solidify, simply place it over very low heat again to remelt.

One at a time, place a cold patty on top of a fork. Submerge the patty in the melted chocolate, then quickly remove. Tap the fork against the pan to shake off any excess chocolate and transfer to a large plate. Repeat with the remaining patties. If there is any chocolate left over, drizzle it on top of the patties to create decorative stripes. Return the patties to the freezer, and freeze until the chocolate has set, 20 to 30 minutes. The patties will remain solid at room temperature but will soften, and are best when served cold. Wrap the patties and store them in the refrigerator, where they will keep for several weeks.

BASIC SUPERFOOD CHOCOLATE

This recipe appeared in my first book, Superfood Kitchen, *and remains a standby recipe for all kinds of superfood treats. To keep the chocolate fully raw, you can use a double boiler to gently melt the cacao butter, but the method below is much quicker and just as gentle.*

MAKES 4.4 OUNCES (BY WEIGHT) / 4 SERVINGS

⅓ cup solid cacao butter, chopped into shavings

5 tablespoons cacao powder

Dash sea salt

2 tablespoons agave nectar

Heat a small saucepan over very low heat. Add the cacao butter and stir to slowly melt into a liquid. The moment all of the shavings have melted in the saucepan, remove it from the heat. Add the cacao powder and salt to the mixture, and use a whisk to thoroughly mix the ingredients. Whisk in the agave nectar. To keep the chocolate warm for dipping, leave it in the warm pan—if it begins to solidify, simply place the pan over very low heat to remelt the chocolate. Or if you want to use the chocolate later, pour it onto a ceramic plate and leave it in the freezer for 30 minutes until it has hardened, then use a dull knife to snap off shards of chocolate. Place them in a resealable container or bag until you are ready to use the chocolate again.

HEMP BUTTER CUPS

If you ever have a craving for chocolate peanut butter cups (and who doesn't?), try these sweet and salty, raw-chocolate-enrobed treats. They are antioxidant rich and offer super benefits, such as skin-friendly fats, complete protein, and low-glycemic sweeteners.

MAKES ABOUT 32 / 16 SERVINGS

1 recipe Basic Superfood Chocolate (page 150), or 1 cup chopped dark chocolate

½ cup Medjool dates (about 7–8 large), pitted

¼ cup unsalted almond butter

⅓ cup shelled hemp seeds

½ teaspoon sea salt

2 tablespoons coconut sugar

1 tablespoon lucuma powder

1 teaspoon maca powder

Line 2 mini muffin tins with 32 mini muffin paper liners or candy wrappers.

In a small saucepan, gently melt the chocolate over very low heat, stirring frequently to avoid burning. Once fully melted, remove chocolate from heat, but keep it in the warm pan to reheat easily should it begin to solidify. Spoon ½ teaspoon of the liquid chocolate into the bottom of each of the wrappers or mini muffin liners to create a bottom layer. Place the tin in the refrigerator for 10 minutes or until chocolate has hardened.

Meanwhile, create the filling: In a food processor, combine the dates, almond butter, hemp seeds, sea salt, coconut sugar, lucuma powder, and maca powder. Process the ingredients into a sticky dough.

To assemble, roll a teaspoon of the filling into a ball and place it on top of the chocolate layer in each of the muffin wrappers or mini muffin liners in the tin. With your fingers, flatten the ball into a layer that is just slightly smaller than the diameter of the chocolate layer. Repeat with the remaining balls of filling. Pour 1 to 2 teaspoons of the melted chocolate on top of each filling so that the chocolate fills up the sides and forms a thin top layer. Place the muffin tin in the refrigerator and cool until the chocolate is solid, 10 to 15 minutes. Serve the Hemp Butter Cups at room temperature or chilled. Store them in a sealed container in the refrigerator or cool environment, where they will last for several weeks.

GINGER RUM FUDGE

This deluxe fudge is definitely a top-shelf treat, and while it may not be for everyday decadence, it is just the thing for those times when you deserve a little something special. Note that this recipe is particularly well served by a high-powered blender. However, you can also make it in a food processor.

MAKES 16 SQUARES / 16 SERVINGS

½ cup finely chopped pecans, divided

½ cup coconut oil, melted

¼ cup cacao butter, melted

½ cup maple syrup

2 tablespoons dark rum

¼ cup lucuma powder

¼ cup cacao powder

1 teaspoon camu berry powder

Pinch sea salt

¾ cup goji berries, divided

¾ cup finely chopped crystallized ginger, divided

Prepare a 6-cup glass dish or loaf pan by greasing the sides and lining the bottom with parchment paper.

In a high-powdered blender or food processor, combine ⅓ cup of the pecans along with the coconut oil, cacao butter, maple syrup, and rum. Blend the ingredients until smooth. Add the lucuma powder, cacao powder, camu berry powder, and sea salt, and blend to incorporate. Add ½ cup of the goji berries and ½ cup crystallized ginger, and blend for a second just to partially chop and mix the ingredients while still leaving plenty of texture. Pour the mixture into the prepared dish, using a small silicone spatula to scrape all of the fudge out of the bottom of the blender and off the blades. Use the same spatula to smooth the surface of the fudge. Scatter the remaining handful of pecans, remaining goji berries, and remaining crystallized ginger over the top of the fudge. Place the fudge in the freezer for 1 hour to fully chill, then cut into 16 squares. Serve cold. Store the fudge in the freezer or refrigerator in a covered container for up to 2 months.

SUPERFOOD BOOST: Add ½ teaspoon spirulina powder for a secret green boost.

COOKIES & PASTRIES

Cookies and pastries certainly don't have the best reputation for being a health food, but in reality they're just a few tweaks away from offering real-deal benefits. Chewy oatmeal cookies, baked breakfast bars, and even crispy rice treats all get the superfood treatment here. Explore some new great uses for super-fruits like fresh berries, super-seeds like hemp and chia, as well as energizing maca root powder to create boosted baked goods that are perfect to reach for any time of the day.

 = FEATURED SUPERFOOD INGREDIENT

 BEAUTY   BONE STRENGTH   HEART HEALTH

 IMMUNITY   LOW CALORIE   PROTEIN

BUTTERSCOTCH-HEMP CRISPY RICE TREATS

Crispy rice treats may be a familiar commodity, but this version is a bounding leap above any "back of the box" recipe. The utterly addictive, mouthwatering butterscotch flavor comes through mainly because of the maca powder, which also makes this such an energizing treat.

MAKES 16 SQUARES / 16 SERVINGS

3 cups crispy brown rice cereal

2 teaspoons maca powder

1½ teaspoons ground cinnamon

¼ cup hemp seeds, divided

½ cup smooth almond butter

⅓ cup maple syrup

3 tablespoons coconut sugar

1 tablespoon coconut oil

⅛ teaspoon sea salt

2 teaspoons vanilla extract

⅓ cup chopped dark chocolate (optional)

Grease a 9 x 9-inch baking pan or line with parchment paper.

In a medium bowl, toss together the crispy rice cereal, maca powder, cinnamon, and 2 tablespoons of the hemp seeds.

In a small saucepan, combine the almond butter, maple syrup, coconut sugar, coconut oil, and sea salt over medium heat. Stirring constantly, cook for 5 minutes, or until ingredients are thoroughly melted. Remove the saucepan from the heat and stir in the vanilla extract.

Pour the hot mixture over the cereal. Mix very well, until the cereal is thoroughly coated. Transfer the mixture to the prepared baking pan, spreading it out evenly. Sprinkle with remaining 2 tablespoons of hemp seeds, and press firmly to compact and flatten the mixture. Refrigerate for a minimum of 1 hour.

Melt the chocolate, if using, in a saucepan over low heat, stirring to keep chocolate from burning. Lightly drizzle the crispy rice treats with the melted chocolate, and refrigerate for a minimum of 20 minutes longer to set. Cut into 16 squares.

SUPERFOOD BOOST: Add 2 tablespoons of chia seeds or flaxseeds for extra fiber and additional omega fats.

GOLDENBERRY MACAROONS

I'm such a sucker for citrus, which is probably why the zingy flavor of goldenberries always blows me away. These unique macaroons offer a real pow of flavor and are exceptionally high in anti-inflammatory nutrients.

MAKES ABOUT 24 MACAROONS / 12 SERVINGS

½ cup raw almonds

½ cup Medjool dates (about 7–8 large), pitted

1 cup dried shredded coconut (unsweetened), divided

¼ teaspoon sea salt

½ teaspoon fresh lemon zest

⅛ teaspoon cayenne pepper

1 teaspoon camu berry powder

2 tablespoons coconut sugar

¼ cup dried goldenberries

In a food processor, combine the almonds and dates and process until a chunky dough forms. Add ¾ cup of the coconut shreds and all the remaining ingredients. Process until the goldenberries have just broken down—do not overprocess or the oils from the nuts will start to release and the cookies will be too dense. Stop the machine and check the consistency: Pinch a small piece of the cookie dough between your fingers—the dough should stick together easily, but still offer a bit of a "crumb." Depending on the natural moisture of the dates, you may need to add a touch of water—1 teaspoon at a time—to get the crumbs to stick together when pinched.

Once the dough is the correct texture, transfer it to a medium bowl. Use a melon baller or tablespoon to scoop up spoonfuls of dough. Pack the dough firmly into the scoop to compact it, then remove the dough from the scoop or spoon to form a cookie. Repeat with the remaining dough. Put the remaining coconut flakes in a shallow bowl and roll the cookies in the coconut until they are completely covered. Macaroons can be enjoyed at room temperature, and will keep for several weeks when stored in an airtight container and refrigerated.

FEEL-GOOD FACT: If you're feeling stressed out, grab some goldenberries! Goldenberries contain stores of stress-reducing B-complex vitamins that support the nervous system, immune system, and adrenal glands.

OATMEAL–MACA COOKIES

Little bites of portable superfood oatmeal—that's what these chewy cookies are! In this recipe, the cookie-jar classic gets a healthy makeover with goji berries replacing raisins and flaxseed powder taking the place of eggs. Maca enhances the flavor of the oats and makes these cookies fully craveable, filling, and energizing.

MAKES 48 COOKIES / 24 SERVINGS

1¾ cups old-fashioned rolled oats*

2 tablespoons maca powder

2 tablespoons flaxseed powder

2 tablespoons lucuma powder

½ cup whole-wheat pastry flour**

½ teaspoon baking powder

½ teaspoon baking soda

½ teaspoon ground cinnamon

¼ teaspoon sea salt

¼ cup coconut oil, melted

⅔ cup coconut sugar

⅔ cup mashed banana (about 2 bananas)

1 teaspoon vanilla extract

½ cup dried goji berries

¼ cup raisins

*Gluten-free rolled oats may be used.

**Use a gluten-free flour blend if desired.

Preheat the oven to 350°F and position 2 racks in the lower third of the oven. Line 2 baking sheets with silicone mats or parchment paper.

In a large bowl, mix together the oats, maca powder, flaxseed powder, lucuma powder, flour, baking powder, baking soda, cinnamon, and sea salt. In another mixing bowl, combine the coconut oil, coconut sugar, banana, and vanilla, and whisk well to combine. Mix the wet mixture into the dry ingredients, then fold in the goji berries and raisins.

To make the cookies, use a melon scoop or tablespoon to drop each scoop of dough onto the prepared baking sheets. Flatten the dough lightly with your fingers—the cookies will not spread while baking. Bake the cookies for 13 to 14 minutes, or until edges begin to turn golden. Let the cookies cool for a couple minutes on the baking sheet, then transfer them to a baking rack to finish cooling.

The cookies can be stored in an airtight container at room temperature for up to 3 days, or frozen for several weeks.

SUPERFOOD BOOST: Add ¼ cup cacao nibs when adding the raisins to increase the mineral content (iron and magnesium). You can also add chocolate chips to make these cookies a little more chocolaty.

HEMP SEED CHOCOLATE CHIP COOKIES

These cookies are not your average chocolate chip cookies with a few seeds thrown in, they are actually made from the superseeds themselves, which are blended right into the dough. With over 3 grams of protein per serving already, I often make them with the Superfood Boost below to boost them further!

MAKES ABOUT 40 COOKIES / 20 SERVINGS

1 cup hemp seeds, divided

¼ cup unsweetened almond milk

2 teaspoons vanilla extract

¼ cup coconut oil, melted

1 cup coconut sugar

1½ cups whole-wheat pastry flour*

1 tablespoon maca powder (optional)

½ teaspoon baking soda

1 teaspoon baking powder

½ teaspoon sea salt

½ cup chocolate chips

⅓ cup cacao nibs

*Use a gluten-free flour blend if desired.

Preheat the oven to 350°F. Line 2 baking sheets with silicone mats or parchment paper.

Pour ¾ cup hemp seeds into a blender (use a small, personal-sized blender if you have one). Add the almond milk and vanilla extract, and blend into a thick paste—the mixture does not need to be perfectly smooth. Use a small silicone spatula to scrape the hemp mixture into a medium bowl. Whisk in the coconut oil and coconut sugar.

In a separate bowl, mix together the flour, maca powder, baking soda, baking powder, and sea salt. Stir in the chocolate chips, cacao nibs, and the remaining ¼ cup hemp seeds, then add the wet mixture to the dry. Mix to form a dough.

Use a melon ball scoop or tablespoon to form balls of dough and place them on the prepared cookie sheets with 1 inch or more between them. Flatten each ball slightly, using your fingertips. Bake the cookies for 12 to 14 minutes, or until they are lightly browned on the bottom. Let the cookies cool on the pan for several minutes before transferring them to a cooling rack.

SUPERFOOD BOOST: Replace ¼ cup of the whole-wheat flour with ¼ cup hemp protein powder (see Resources Guide on page 209). This simple superfood swap adds an additional gram of protein to each and every serving!

ORANGE GEM MINI MUFFINS

Do mini muffins taste better? I'm not sure why they technically would, but I always feel like they just do. This is a great little "coffee and tea" muffin that's slightly orangey in flavor, not too over-the-top sweet, just moist enough, and tucks away all kinds of flavorful and healthy ingredient gems, such as goji berries, ginger, apple, and hemp seeds. While these muffins are wonderful enjoyed fresh out of the oven, they're also a welcome surprise in kids' lunchboxes, used as a preworkout snack, or even a healthy aid for a case of midnight munchies. Stored in a zip lock bag or sealed container in a dark place, they'll stay nice and moist and last up to 1 week.

MAKES 24 MINI MUFFINS / 12 SERVINGS

- 2 tablespoons ground flaxseed powder
- ⅓ cup apple juice
- 1½ cups whole-wheat pastry flour*
- 1 teaspoon baking powder
- 1 teaspoon baking soda
- ½ teaspoon sea salt
- 3 tablespoons hemp seeds
- ⅓ cup applesauce
- 3 tablespoons coconut oil, melted
- ¼ cup agave nectar
- 1 teaspoon vanilla extract
- 1 teaspoon fresh orange zest
- 2 tablespoons crystallized ginger, finely minced
- ⅓ cup dried goji berries
- ¼ cup fresh apple, finely minced

*Use a gluten-free flour blend if desired.

Preheat the oven to 350°F. Lightly grease a 24-cup mini muffin pan or use paper liners.

In a small bowl, mix together the flaxseed powder and apple juice. Let stand for 15 minutes to allow the mixture to thicken into a gel.

In a large bowl, mix together the flour, baking powder, baking soda, sea salt, and hemp seeds.

In a medium bowl, whisk together the gelled flaxseed mixture with the applesauce, coconut oil, agave nectar, vanilla, and orange zest. Mix in the minced ginger, goji berries, and apple. Pour the liquid mixture into the dry ingredients and mix until just combined—do not overmix. Batter will be thick.

Distribute the batter among the muffin cups and lightly smooth the tops. Bake for 16 to 18 minutes or until golden brown. Let the muffins cool slightly before popping them out of the pan onto a cooling rack. Muffins can be stored in an airtight container or bag for up to 1 week.

SUPERFOOD BOOST: Add 2 tablespoons chia seeds when mixing together the dry ingredients to further increase the fiber, calcium, and iron in this recipe.

RASPBERRY QUICK BREAD

This rustic loaf is a cross between bread and pound cake and manages to remain nice and moist while still keeping the overall fat content in check. To give this delicious quick bread maximum raspberry flavor, some of the berries are blended into the dough, while others are left to soften during baking, which give the bread lots of little jammy flavor pockets. This is one of those breads that continues to improve as it ages and tastes even better on the second day.

MAKES 1 LOAF / 8 SERVINGS

⅓ cup apple juice

3 tablespoons flaxseed powder

2 cups fresh raspberries, divided

¾ cup coconut sugar

¼ cup melted coconut oil

1 teaspoon fresh lemon zest

1 teaspoon fresh lemon juice

1 teaspoon vanilla extract

1½ cups whole-wheat pastry flour*

¼ cup lucuma powder, plus extra for garnish

1 teaspoon baking soda

2 teaspoons baking powder

½ teaspoon sea salt

*Use a gluten-free flour blend if desired.

Preheat oven to 350°F. Lightly grease a 9- by 5-inch loaf pan with coconut oil.

In a blender, add the apple juice, flaxseed powder, and 1 cup of the raspberries, and blend until smooth. Pour into a medium bowl and set aside for 5 to 10 minutes to allow the ingredients to gel. Once slightly thickened, whisk in the coconut sugar, coconut oil, lemon zest, lemon juice, and vanilla.

In another medium bowl, mix together the flour, lucuma powder, baking soda, baking powder, and sea salt. Add the wet mixture to the dry and mix until just combined—do not overmix (batter will be very thick). Fold in the remaining raspberries, smashing them lightly to create large chunks of fruit.

Scrape the batter into the prepared pan and lightly smooth the top. Bake the bread in the center of the oven for 45 to 50 minutes, or until a toothpick inserted in the middle of the loaf comes out clean. Transfer the loaf to a cooling rack and let it cool for 10 minutes, then turn the bread out onto the rack. Garnish the top with a light dusting of lucuma powder, then cut it into slices and serve.

Once fully cooled, the bread may be wrapped tightly in plastic wrap and refrigerated for up to 1 week, or frozen in plastic and foil for up to 1 month.

MACA MOCHURROS
(AKA MOCHI CHURROS)

If there can be a Cronut—a croissant-donut hybrid—then there's certainly room in this world for mochurros, my proud crossbreed of mochi (an ingenious puff pastry–like product from Japan), and churros (of Mexican cuisine and state fair fame).

MAKES 9 12-INCH MOCHURROS / 4–6 SERVINGS

1 package (12.5-ounce) mochi*

1 tablespoon coconut oil, melted

¼ cup coconut sugar

4 teaspoons ground cinnamon

1 teaspoon maca powder

⅛ teaspoon sea salt

*For best results use a plain variety of mochi. Superfood varieties or cinnamon-raisin flavor may also be used if available.

SUPERFOOD TIP: Mochi can be found in most natural food stores in the refrigerated or frozen section. See the Resources Guide on page 209 for brand suggestions.

Preheat the oven to 450°F. Line 2 baking sheets with silicone mats or parchment paper.

Use a chef's knife to trim the side of one of the long ends of the mochi block to create one flat edge. With the flat edge facing you, carefully slice the mochi lengthwise into ¼-inch strips.

With a pastry brush, lightly brush both sides of each mochi strip with a little of the melted oil. Arrange the strips in pairs so that their flat edges are touching each other end-to-end to create (9 total) 12-inch strips that will become conjoined when baked (make sure no other edges are close to touching, or else they will stick, too). Reserve the remaining melted oil.

Place the baking sheets with the mochi in the oven and bake for 10 minutes, or until the mochi is puffy and crisp.

While the mochi is baking, pour the sugar, cinnamon, maca powder, and sea salt into a pie pan or other shallow baking dish. Mix well to combine and shake the dish to create a flat layer of seasoning.

After the mochi is finished baking, remove it from the oven. One at a time, lightly paint the exterior of the mochi with coconut oil (using tongs, if needed, to handle the mochi while it is hot), then roll mochi in the spiced sugar to lightly cover. Transfer mochi to a plate. Repeat with the remaining strips. Mochurros are best served immediately, but will retain a semi-crisp texture for about a day.

LAVENDER GRAHAM CRACKERS

Lavender likes to play coy: Use too much and you'll have edible soap, but add just enough and your delighted response will be ". . . can't put my finger on it, but there's something unexpectedly enchanting about what I'm eating." Not to mention the wonderful nuttiness of teff is pretty hard to resist! A bonus: While these crackers are baking, your house will smell like absolute heaven on earth.

MAKES 48 CRACKERS / 12 SERVINGS

2 cups teff flour

½ cup coconut sugar

¼ cup lucuma powder

¼ cup flaxseed powder

1 teaspoon baking soda

1 teaspoon sea salt

2 teaspoons dried lavender blossoms, minced

1 tablespoon vanilla extract

¼ cup coconut oil

¼ cup maple syrup

⅓ cup unsweetened almond milk

SUPERFOOD TIP: If you have access to fresh lavender flowers, use them! Just be sure to use only the floral parts, and chop them very finely prior to adding them to the food processor.

In a food processor, combine the teff flour, coconut sugar, lucuma powder, flaxseed powder, baking soda and sea salt. Add the remaining ingredients and process until a dough has formed (dough will be firm and slightly sticky). Divide the dough in half and shape it into two balls, cover them loosely, and refrigerate for 1 hour.

Preheat the oven to 325°F. Lightly flour two silicone baking mats with additional teff flour or flour of choice (or use two pieces of lightly floured parchment paper the same size as your baking sheet), place a ball of dough on top of a sheet, and lay a piece of parchment paper on top of the dough. Roll out the dough into an 8- by 10-inch rectangle. Place it on a baking sheet and carefully remove the top layer of parchment. Lightly cut the dough into 2-inch squares with a pizza cutter, then use a fork to score each square with decorative dots. Repeat this process with the second half of the dough and place it on a second baking sheet. Bake the crackers on the center rack of the oven, rotating the pans halfway through, for 18 to 22 minutes, or until crackers are dried but not burned.

Remove the crackers from the oven and cool for 5 minutes, then place crackers on a wire rack to finish cooling and become crisper. The crackers will keep in an airtight container for 2 weeks.

Serving suggestions: *Enjoy these fragrant crackers with a cold glass of almond milk or a warm cup of tea.*

STRAWBERRY PEACH CRISP

Have you ever known a naturally beautiful woman who insists upon always covering herself in an exceedingly thick mask of make-up? If so, you can understand exactly how I feel about the tradition of loading baked fruit crisps with tons of sugar. Ripe fruit really needs so very little to heighten its treat factor, especially when it is transformed into such syrupy-soft pleasure when it is baked (and topped simply with crunchy oats). You can easily prep the ramekins ahead of time and store them in the refrigerator so you can just pop them in the oven whenever.

MAKES 4 SERVINGS

⅓ cup dried goldenberries

1 cup hot water

¼ cup fresh orange juice

2 tablespoons arrowroot powder (optional)*

1 teaspoon freshly grated lemon zest

¾ teaspoon ground cinnamon, divided

1 cup strawberries, trimmed and quartered

1½ cup peaches, cut into ½-inch wedges

½ cup rolled oats**

2 tablespoons coconut sugar

4 teaspoons coconut oil, melted

Coconut yogurt, for serving (optional)

Preheat the oven to 375°F. Coat 4 5-ounce ramekins with cooking spray.

Place the goldenberries in a medium bowl and pour the hot water on top. Let the berries sit for 20 minutes to soften, then drain. Add the orange juice, arrowroot powder if using, lemon zest, and ¼ teaspoon of the cinnamon to the drained goldenberries and mix well. Fold in the strawberries and peaches.

In a separate bowl, mix together the oats, coconut sugar, coconut oil, and remaining ½ teaspoon cinnamon.

Fill ramekins with the fruit mixture, then sprinkle the oats on top. Bake for 20 to 25 minutes or until the top is golden brown and the fruit is bubbling. Remove the ramekins from the oven and cool for a minimum of 15 minutes. To serve, top the crisp with a dollop of coconut yogurt, if using. Fruit crisps may be served warm or at room temperature. Extra ramekins can be stored in the refrigerator for several days.

* Arrowroot powder helps thicken the fruit mixture when baked, without adding sugar (it's virtually flavorless).

**Gluten-free rolled oats may be used.

CRANBERRY–GOJI SQUARES

Hooray for "baked goodies" that don't require any baking—and take less than 10 minutes to prepare! I make these vitamin-loaded, moist yet crunchy squares for my pastry-loving family all year, especially when it's "I wish we had air-conditioning" weather.

MAKES 16 BARS / 16 SERVINGS

¾ cup raw cashews

½ cup dried shredded coconut (unsweetened)

¼ cup coconut sugar

¼ cup lucuma powder

1 tablespoon ground flaxseed powder

½ teaspoon camu berry powder

1 teaspoon ground cinnamon

⅛ teaspoon sea salt

¼ cup unsweetened applesauce

1 teaspoon vanilla extract

2½ cups crispy brown rice cereal, divided

½ cup dried goji berries

½ cup dried cranberries (fruit juice–sweetened, preferably)

⅓ cup raw pecans

Place the cashews in a food processor and grind into a coarse flour. Add the coconut shreds, coconut sugar, lucuma powder, flaxseed powder, camu berry powder, cinnamon, and sea salt, and blend to combine. Add the applesauce and vanilla and blend to form a wet dough. Add 2 cups of the brown rice cereal and process until cereal is ground into fine crumbs. Add the remaining ½ cup of cereal, goji berries, cranberries, and pecans, and blend just for a moment to coarsely chop the last round of ingredients, but retain most of the texture.

Transfer the dough to a 9- by 9-inch pan lined with parchment paper. Use your hands to firmly press the dough into a flat layer, compressing it as much as possible to ensure that it is compact. Using the edges of the parchment, carefully lift the contents out of the pan, and set it on a flat surface. For a more aesthetic product (though it's not necessary), you can set a second sheet of parchment paper on top of the square and use a rolling pin to gently roll the top perfectly flat. Use a chef's knife to carefully cut 16 squares, and serve them at room temperature.

Covered tightly, the squares will keep for several days at room temperature, or 1 week refrigerated.

SUPERFOOD BOOST: Bring out those powders! You can easily add a teaspoon of acai berry powder, maqui berry powder, or even wheatgrass powder when combining the dry ingredients.

APRICOT QUINOA SQUARES

Lightly toasted quinoa offers a delectable nutty flavor, which is showcased perfectly in these protein-packed, mineral-rich, toothsome treats. And with such a lovely sweet 'n' spice allure, you'd never guess these squares were sweetened 100% with fruit.

MAKES 16 SQUARES / 16 SERVINGS

¾ cup Medjool dates (about 11–12 large), pitted

⅔ cup apple juice

1 tablespoon vanilla extract

¼ cup chia seeds, divided

3 tablespoons coconut oil

1½ cups quinoa flakes

1½ cup coarsely chopped raw walnuts

¼ teaspoon sea salt

½ teaspoon ground cinnamon

½ teaspoon ground anise

1 cup coarsely chopped dried Turkish apricots (no sulfites/sugar added),

½ cup dried white mulberries

Preheat the oven to 350°F. Lightly spray an 8-inch square pan with oil.

In a food processor, combine the dates, apple juice, and vanilla, and let sit for 10 minutes to soften, then blend until smooth. Transfer the mixture to a small bowl, scraping the blender very well with a silicone spatula or spoon to remove all the contents. Mix in 2 tablespoons of the chia seeds and stir the puree well to avoid chia clumps. Set aside for another 10 minutes to allow the chia to thicken.

Meanwhile, melt the coconut oil in a large skillet over medium heat. Add the quinoa flakes, walnuts, and sea salt. Cook, stirring frequently, for 3 to 4 minutes until the quinoa and nuts are fragrant. Add the cinnamon and anise and cook for 30 seconds more, then remove the pan from the heat and immediately transfer the contents to a large bowl. Mix in the apricots, mulberries, chia mixture, and the remaining 2 tablespoons of chia seeds. Stir well to distribute the ingredients, which should come together as a chunky dough.

Transfer the dough to the prepared baking pan and press it down firmly into a flat layer. Bake for 30 minutes, or until edges turn golden. Remove the pan from the oven and let cool for a minimum of 20 minutes. Cut into 16 squares.

When fully cool, wrap tightly in plastic wrap or sealable container. May be stored for up to 1 week at room temperature, 2 weeks refrigerated, or several months in the freezer.

PUMPKIN CHEESECAKE SQUARES

Although there are many healthy benefits here, the biggest secret ingredient is really the chia seeds, which help firm up the cheesecake filling while reducing the fat content. So go ahead: Enjoy this festive, no-bake, low-sugar mousse-like cheesecake without any guilt. Surprisingly, it's even better the next day.

MAKES 8 2-INCH SQUARES / 8 SERVINGS

1 cup raw almonds

½ cup Medjool dates (about 7–8 large), pitted

2 tablespoons vanilla protein powder

1 teaspoon vanilla extract

1 teaspoon sea salt

1 cup pumpkin puree

½ cup coconut butter, melted

1 tablespoon cacao butter, melted

¼ cup chia seeds

¼ cup coconut sugar

3 drops liquid stevia

1½ cups almond milk

1 tablespoon pumpkin pie spice

1 teaspoon cinnamon powder

½ teaspoon ginger powder

1 teaspoon apple cider vinegar

Yacon Caramel Sauce (opposite)

Sliced almonds

To make the crust: In a food processor, grind 1 cup almonds, dates, protein powder, vanilla, and sea salt together into a coarse "dough." Test the consistency by pinching the dough between 2 fingers—the dough should stick together easily, while maintaining a light crumb. If dough is too dry, blend in a little water, 1 teaspoon at a time. If the dough is too wet, blend in a few extra almonds. Turn the dough out into a springform 9-inch square pan (a round springform pan is okay too; you'll just want to cut wedges instead of squares). Alternatively, divide the mixture among mini cheesecake pans to make mini pumpkin cheesecakes instead of squares, and press the dough firmly into a flat layer to cover the bottom of the pan.

To make the filling: In a blender, combine the pumpkin puree, coconut butter, cacao butter, chia seeds, coconut sugar, stevia, almond milk, spices, and apple cider vinegar. Blend until completely smooth. Pour on top of prepared crust. Refrigerate 8 hours or overnight to set the filling. (To speed up the process, cheesecake may be frozen for 2 hours, then defrosted in the refrigerator for 1 to 2 hours.)

To serve, remove from pan and cut the cheesecake into 8 squares. Drizzle the top with Yacon Caramel Sauce (opposite)and sprinkle with sliced almonds.

YACON CARAMEL SAUCE

MAKES ½ CUP

⅓ cup yacon syrup

3 tablespoons roasted smooth almond butter (premixed)

1 tablespoon cacao butter, melted

¼ teaspoon vanilla extract

¼ teaspoon sea salt

In a small bowl, mix together the yacon syrup and almond butter with a fork until smooth. Add the cacao butter, vanilla, and sea salt and stir to incorporate. The mixture will remain soft while at room temperature, but will firm up when cooled.

FROZEN TREATS

No need to wait until dessert, these aren't your average frozen treats! Ice cream bonbons are reimagined, and made with recharging maca and cacao; and adventurously-flavored popsicles are stealthfully infused with cleansing wheatgrass. And since a freezer preserves food, frozen superfood snacks can be conveniently tucked away for weeks or months at a time, ready whenever you are.

 = FEATURED SUPERFOOD INGREDIENT

 BEAUTY BONE STRENGTH HEART HEALTH

 IMMUNITY LOW CALORIE PROTEIN

LEMON–GOJI ICEBOX COOKIES

To make these buttery cookies, all you need is the freezer—no oven! The result?
Irresistible treats that contain anti-aging antioxidants and healthy fats.

MAKES 18 COOKIES / 9 SERVINGS

1 cup raw cashews

1 cup dried white mulberries

¼ cup coconut sugar

¼ teaspoon sea salt

1 tablespoon fresh lemon zest

2 tablespoons coconut oil

2 tablespoons dried goji berries

In a food processor, grind the cashews and mulberries into a coarse flour. Add the coconut sugar and sea salt, and combine. While the machine is running, add the lemon zest and coconut oil, and process until a sticky dough has formed. Add the goji berries and pulse just a few times—enough to chop up the goji berries, but still retain a few large pieces.

Place a large sheet of plastic wrap on a flat surface and put the cookie dough on top of it. Shape the dough into a compact oval. Seal the plastic wrap around the dough, then gently roll the dough into a 10-inch-long cookie log. Place it in the freezer for 10 minutes to chill slightly.

Remove the plastic wrap from the dough, and carefully cut it into ¼-inch rounds—if a cookie breaks apart, simply press it back together. Put the cookies on a baking sheet in a flat layer, cover them with plastic wrap, then return the cookies to the freezer for a minimum of 30 minutes. These icebox cookies are best when served chilled; to store, cover and keep in the freezer.

Variation: *Use dried blueberries or dried goldenberries in place of the goji berries.*

ALMOND & BLUEBERRY SOFT-SERVE SANDWICHES

The refreshing temperature of these freezer-friendly snacks isn't the only cool thing about this treat—each "sandwich" may seem decadent—yet, in actuality, it is primarily a serving of fruit and nuts, with very few other ingredients. The cookie crust is like very lightly sweetened almond sandies, and the creamy center is vibrantly fruity—a composition of natural flavors that truly shine proudly in this recipe. For lazy days, you can also simply serve the soft-serve and cookies together in a bowl!

MAKES 12 SANDWICHES / 12 SERVINGS

2 cups blanched almond flour

½ cup quinoa flakes

⅓ cup coconut sugar

½ teaspoon baking soda

¼ teaspoon sea salt

½ cup coconut oil, melted

¼ cup maple syrup

1 teaspoon lemon zest

1 tablespoon lemon juice

1 teaspoon vanilla extract

4 frozen bananas (see page 178), sliced into 1-inch rounds

1 cup frozen blueberries

½ cup unsweetened almond milk

1 teaspoon ground cinnamon

¼ cup hemp seeds (optional)

First, make the cookies: Preheat the oven to 350°F. In a medium bowl, mix together the almond flour, quinoa flakes, coconut sugar, baking soda, and sea salt. In a small bowl, combine the coconut oil, maple syrup, lemon zest, lemon juice, and vanilla extract, and whisk well. Pour the wet ingredients into the dry and stir to combine. Knead the dough a couple of times to further mix and compact, then form the dough into 2 balls. Sandwich a ball between 2 silicone baking mats or pieces of parchment paper and roll out into a ¼-inch layer. Peel off the top mat or paper and use a 2-inch round cookie cutter to stamp circles in the dough. Strip away the excess dough around the circles and transfer the mat with the cookies to a baking sheet. Repeat with the remaining ball and use the collected extra dough to create one last batch of cookies. Bake cookies on the center rack of the oven for 9 to 12 minutes, or until the bottoms begin to turn golden. Let the cookies rest on the baking sheet to cool and firm up for 10 minutes before removing. Transfer cooled cookies to a plate, cover with plastic or aluminum, and freeze until ready for assembly.

To make the soft serve filling, place the frozen bananas and blueberries in a food processor. Pulse the machine several times

to create chunks of fruit the size of large gravel. Add the almond milk and cinnamon, and process until a stiff soft-serve begins to form—you can leave some whole blueberries and unmixed banana in for texture and visual appeal or whip the mixture smooth. The soft serve will melt quickly, so keep it in the freezer until ready to assemble the sandwiches.

To assemble, place a small scoop of the soft-serve between two cookies and press together lightly to form a sandwich. Sprinkle the sides lightly with hemp seeds, if using. Repeat to form the remaining sandwiches. Freeze the sandwiches for at least one hour before serving.

Kept in a sealed container in the freezer, sandwiches can be stored for several weeks.

FROZEN BANANAS

Make a big batch of frozen bananas so you'll have this versatile ingredient on hand for all types of treats—from desserts to smoothies. Here are some tips:

- Use the brownest, ripest bananas you can find—they become truly delicious when frozen.
- Before freezing, remove the peel and cut the fruit into pieces. Place them in a flat layer inside a resealable plastic freezer bag. This retains the freshness and makes the banana pieces easier to work with.
- Cut the bananas into a consistent size to simplify measuring. For example, you might decide to always cut bananas into sixths, so when a recipe calls for "one frozen banana," you'll know how many pieces to include for one banana.

BANANA BONBONS

Simply freezing bananas turns them into an ice cream–like treat—amazing! I love that this quick recipe is impressive enough to serve at a dinner party, yet is equally welcomed by kids.

MAKES ABOUT 24 BONBONS / 12 SERVINGS

3 frozen bananas (page 178)

1 batch Basic Superfood Chocolate (page 150)

1 tablespoon coconut oil

2 tablespoons hemp seeds (optional)

Slice the bananas into 1-inch rounds and place them back in the freezer until ready for assembly.

In a small saucepan over very low heat, make or remelt Basic Superfood Chocolate and add the coconut oil. Whisk to combine, then remove the chocolate from the heat, but keep it in the warm pan. Pour the hemp seeds into a small bowl and have a fork and knife on standby. Line a plate or tray that fits in your freezer with parchment paper.

To assemble with best results, touch the bananas as little as possible, using the fork and knife rather than your fingers. Load a banana slice on the prongs of a fork and place it in the chocolate. Working quickly, roll the slice around to coat all sides in chocolate, and remove with the fork. Use the knife to slide the bonbon off of the fork onto the prepared plate and lightly sprinkle the bonbon with hemp seeds—the chocolate will begin to harden almost immediately. Repeat with remaining slices. Return the bonbons to the freezer for 20 minutes, then serve. Bonbons may be stored in a sealed container or resealable bag for up to 2 months.

Variation: *For an extra-creamy, even more delicious version, make a triple-layer bonbon by creating an inside layer of nut butter. You can use any of the superfood recipes in this book (see recipes for Power Seed Butter on page 116 and Maca Cashew Butter on page 115) or your own nut or seed butter of choice—get creative!*

SALTED CHOCOLATE
AND MACA ICE CREAM BONBONS

Whenever my attitude suggested laziness, as a child, my family's recurring joke (much to my chagrin) was that I couldn't just "sit around, watch the soaps, and eat bonbons all day"—which made me grit my little-kid teeth, because I never watched soap operas, nor had I ever tried a bonbon. So, a few years back, when I finally acquired my first, luxurious, creamy ice cream ball coated with snappy chocolate, let's just say it's a good thing the experience happened well into my adult years, or else my family's joke may have been right on the mark. This recipe for superfood-infused bonbons is more than just utterly unreal in the taste department, it is, quite literally, the good-mood-maker too: Cacao, maca powder, healthy fats, and minerals have all been linked to enhancing mood, brain health, and increasing serotonin. Although these bonbons take a couple days to create, you can make the ice cream in advance, and reduce the actual time spent in the kitchen making the bonbons, to less than an hour. File this recipe under "worth it."

MAKES 30 BONBONS / 15 SERVINGS

1 cup raw cashews

1 cup coconut water

½ banana, peeled

¼ cup maple syrup

✳ 2 tablespoons maca powder

1 teaspoon vanilla extract

✳ 1 batch Basic Superfood Chocolate (page 150)

1 tablespoon coconut oil

Flaked sea salt, for sprinkling

To make the ice cream, blend the cashews, coconut water, banana, maple syrup, maca powder, and vanilla in a high-powered blender or food processor until completely smooth. For best results, pour into an ice cream maker and follow the manufacturer's instructions. (Alternately, simply transfer the mixture to a container and freeze, covered, until frozen through, churning the mixture by hand about every 30 minutes for 3 hours to help create a fluffier ice cream.) Regardless of method, freeze the ice cream overnight to fully solidify.

Line 3 small plates (which can fit on the racks in your freezer) with parchment paper. Tightly pack a melon ball scoop, small ice cream scoop, or tablespoon with balls of ice cream and place balls on a prepared plate. Note that the ice cream should be stiff but scoopable—if it's too hard, let it soften slightly at room temperature for 1 to 2 minutes, but do not let it melt. When a plate holds 10 balls, return it to the freezer. Repeat with the remaining ice cream.

When all the ice cream balls are frozen, make or remelt Basic Superfood Chocolate, and add the coconut oil in a small saucepan over very low heat. Whisk to combine. Once liquefied, remove the chocolate from heat but keep it in the warm pan. Pour a little flaked sea salt onto a small plate, and have a toothpick, a spoon, and a fork on standby.

To assemble the bonbons, remove a plate of ice cream balls from the freezer. Working very quickly, insert the toothpick into the flat bottom of a ball. Using the toothpick, hold a bonbon over the saucepan, and spoon melted chocolate over the entire surface of the ice cream, rotating it to spread the chocolate more quickly. Once the bonbon is coated, sprinkle the top with a light dusting of sea salt. Use the prongs of the fork to release the bonbon from the toothpick back to the cold plate. Repeat until all ice cream balls are coated with chocolate, then return the plate to the freezer. Continue with the remaining balls, one plate at a time.

Freeze the bonbons until firm, about 30 minutes, then serve. Store the bonbons in a sealable container or resealable bag—they will keep for 2 to 3 months.

SUPERFOOD TIP: Flaked sea salt is different from regular sea salt—due to its thin composition, flaked sea salt "melts" and exposes its flavor more quickly than regular sea salt. For brand recommendations, see page 209—one box of flaked sea salt will last an extremely long time, and it will enhance the taste of everything you make, from desserts to sandwiches.

WATERMELON GOJI POPSICLES

On a brutally hot summer evening—the kind that refuses to offer any relief, even after dark—my boyfriend and I stumbled upon the deep pleasures of frozen watermelon—a cooling, sweet, electrolyte-filled snack that slowly lets juice drift onto your tongue at the perfect rate—just enough to keep your taste buds continually expectant. Although "watermelon for dinner?" is now an ongoing joke at home, frozen watermelon snacks have nevertheless become a summer mainstay.

MAKES ABOUT 8 POPSICLES / 8 SERVINGS

4 cups cubed seedless watermelon, rind removed, divided

1 tablespoon agave nectar (optional)

3 tablespoons fresh lime juice

⅓ cup dried goji berries

1 teaspoon freshly grated lime zest

Liquid stevia, to taste

Put 2 cups of the watermelon, agave nectar, and lime juice in a blender and liquefy. Add the goji berries and process until smooth. Add the remaining watermelon and the lime zest, blending for a moment to combine while retaining a little bit of texture. Taste for sweetness and add a little stevia to enhance the flavor (around 10 drops)—the mix should taste quite sweet. Pour the liquid into popsicle molds and freeze until hard, about 3 hours. The popsicles will keep for a couple of weeks, covered and frozen.

FEEL-GOOD FACT: Watermelon is one of the best sources of electrolytes – an essential collection of minerals the body relies upon for all kinds of cellular and nerve function. Since electrolytes are often lost during heat exposure through sweat, rehydrating with cooling watermelon is beneficial on every level.

JALAPEÑO POPSICLES

You read correctly: not jalapeño poppers, jalapeño popsicles. Eating these sweet pops feels downright flirty, with the spicy heat of the pepper dancing with the ice-cold pop for an exciting taste-bud sensation. If you dare to amp things up another notch, keep a couple of the jalapeño seeds on hand to add to your blend. In addition to being straight-up fun, this recipe helps maintain clear skin and detoxifies.

MAKES ABOUT 8 POPSICLES / 8 SERVINGS

1½ cups cucumber, peeled and chopped

1½ cups coconut water

¼ cup fresh lemon juice

½ green jalapeño pepper, seeds removed

½ teaspoon wheatgrass powder

2 tablespoons agave nectar

Liquid stevia, to taste

In a blender, combine the cucumber, coconut water, lemon juice, jalapeño, wheatgrass powder, and agave nectar. Blend until smooth. Over a mixing bowl, pour the mixture through a fine-mesh sieve or a couple of layers of cheesecloth to strain out any excess fibers. Taste, and add stevia (about 20 drops) to enhance sweetness. Pour the mixture into popsicle molds and freeze until hard, about 3 hours. The popsicles will keep for several weeks, covered and frozen.

> **FEEL-GOOD FACT:** Wheatgrass has been shown to reduce the harmful side effects of chemotherapy without altering the effectiveness of treatment. Thanks to its high concentration of vitamins and minerals, it not only detoxifies, it actually replenishes the body with vital nutrition at the same time.

CACAO ICE CREAM

Cacao offers a lighter flavor than cocoa, which makes this ice cream delicate, oh-so creamy, and light. With its low sugar footprint, I never feel guilty about sitting down with a scoop, which I love to top with fresh berries from the farmer's market (especially raspberries!) if I have them on hand. Note that the vodka helps reduce the iciness of the ice cream, improving the texture, but it may be omitted.

MAKES 3 CUPS / 6 SERVINGS

1 15-ounce can full-fat coconut milk (do not substitute with light)

1 frozen banana (page 178)

2 tablespoons agave nectar

2 teaspoons vanilla extract

⅓ cup cacao powder

1 tablespoon vodka (optional)

Place all the ingredients in a blender and blend until very smooth and creamy. For best results, pour the mixture into an ice cream maker and follow the manufacturer's instructions. (Alternatively, simply transfer the mixture to a container and freeze, covered, until frozen through, churning the mixture by hand, every 30 minutes or so, for 3 hours to help create a fluffier ice cream.) Store the ice cream in the freezer, and let it soften at room temperature for a couple of minutes before serving.

SUPERFOOD BOOST: Add 2 teaspoons of maca to the blend before freezing for an extra depth of flavor and additional energizing properties.

GOLDENBERRY KOMBUCHA SORBET

Kombucha is a fizzy, fermented drink made from tea and cultures. Its snappy flavor (and digestive benefits) make it a welcome addition to superfood frozen desserts like this one. Combine it with a loud-mouthed flavor like goldenberry, and you have a surprisingly sophisticated frozen fruit treat. For a dramatic serving presentation, offset the sunset-colored blush from the strawberries with a topping of crushed green pistachios in a fancy parfait dish.

MAKES 3 CUPS / 6 SERVINGS

⅓ cup dried goldenberries

1 cup hot water

1 cup frozen mango chunks

1 cup frozen strawberries

1½ cups unflavored kombucha

2 tablespoons yacon syrup or agave nectar

⅛ teaspoon guar gum (optional)

Place the goldenberries in a small bowl and cover with the hot water. Let the berries sit for 15 minutes to soften, then drain the water.

Place the drained goldenberries, along with all the remaining ingredients, in a blender, and blend until smooth. For best results, pour the mixture into an ice cream maker and follow the manufacturer's instructions. (Alternatively, simply transfer the mixture to a container and freeze, covered, until frozen through, churning the mixture by hand, every 30 minutes or so, for 3 hours to help create a fluffier sorbet.) Store the sorbet in the freezer, and let it soften at room temperature for a couple of minutes before serving.

SUPERFOOD BOOST: Add ¼ teaspoon camu berry powder while blending together the ingredients for extra vitamin C, or add 1 teaspoon maqui berry powder for additional heart-healthy antioxidants.

SECRET MINT CHIP ICE CREAM

In my book Superfood Smoothies, *one of the most popular recipes is a mint chip smoothie that tastes so good it's almost like ice cream. Here, we have a superfood ice cream that is so nutritious it could almost be mistaken for a superfood smoothie! And . . . since you won't taste the spinach and spirulina in this recipe—I like to keep their healthy green goodness a secret—no one will know. For the best results, use regular canned coconut milk, not the reduced fat variety.*

MAKES 1 QUART / 16 SERVINGS

⁂ ⅓ cup cacao nibs, or finely chopped dark chocolate

1⅓ cups canned full-fat coconut milk

1 cup coconut water

⁂ 2 packed cups baby spinach

⁂ ¾ packed cup fresh mint leaves, minced

2 cups frozen bananas, chopped (page 178)

2 teaspoons vanilla extract

¼ teaspoon mint extract

⁂ ½ teaspoon spirulina powder

2 tablespoons agave nectar

20 drops liquid stevia, or to taste

In a spice mill or mini blender, briefly blend the cacao nibs into smaller sandy bits. Set aside.

In a blender, puree coconut milk, coconut water, spinach, and mint leaves until very smooth. Add the frozen bananas, vanilla extract, mint extract, spirulina powder, agave nectar, and stevia, then blend to incorporate. For best results, pour the mixture into an ice cream maker and follow the manufacturer's instructions. Add the ground cacao nibs to the machine a couple minutes before the ice cream is frozen through. (Alternatively, simply transfer the mixture to a container and freeze, covered, until fully frozen through, churning the mixture by hand, every 30 minutes or so, for 3 hours to help create a fluffier ice cream. The cacao nibs can be mixed in 30 minutes after freezing, once the mixture has begun to thicken.) Store the ice cream in the freezer, and let it soften at room temperature for 5 to 10 minutes before serving.

SUPERFOOD BOOST: Add ½ teaspoon camu berry powder for extra vitamin C.

KOMBUCHA ICE CREAM FLOAT

A long time ago, I discovered that combining bubbly kombucha with vanilla extract and a little stevia gives cream soda a real run for its money. So of course, like any dedicated sweet tooth, I thought of ice cream floats. And sure enough, kombucha makes absolutely outstanding ones. Kombucha ice cream floats—simply assembled with fruit and ice cream—are great to serve at dinner parties, especially when you top them off, dramatically, with foamy kombucha right at the table. However, since all of the ingredients in this ice cream float are so healthy, you don't have to wait for a dinner party to enjoy them. You can whip up this guilt-free treat anytime for a little pick-me-up!

MAKES 1 FLOAT / 1 SERVING

1 cup unflavored kombucha

½ teaspoon vanilla extract

5 drops liquid stevia

⅓ cup frozen raspberries

⅓ cup Cacao Ice Cream (page 184), or your favorite chocolate or vanilla ice cream

In a measuring cup with a spout, stir together the kombucha, vanilla extract, and stevia.

In a 16-ounce serving glass or mason jar, place a spoonful of raspberries, followed by a spoonful of cacao ice cream, and layer each of these ingredients about 4 times. Slowly pour in the kombucha—it will foam up immediately but settle quickly. Enjoy this ice cream float right away!

> **FEEL-GOOD FACT:** Most people use kombucha as an excellent elixir for digestive support, but in traditional Japanese culture, Kombucha tea is also used to give the kidneys a healthy boost, as well as the urinary system, the reproductive system, and pancreatic functioning.

BLOOD ORANGE & THYME GRANITA

Most granita recipes call for a heavy load of white sugar, but it's surprisingly easy to transform them into a much more healthful treat using stevia, a little agave, and natural fruit. Blood oranges create a stunning color here, but if they're not in season, Navel oranges or even grapefruits will do the trick just fine.

MAKES 1 QUART / 4 SERVINGS

7–8 blood oranges, juiced (about 2 cups of juice)

1 cup coconut water

6 sprigs fresh thyme

2 tablespoons agave nectar

1 teaspoon vanilla extract

¼ teaspoon camu berry powder

1 tablespoon vodka (optional)

Liquid stevia, to taste

Use a paring knife to slice off the zest in large strips from one of the oranges. Set the strips aside. Juice the peeled orange, as well as the remaining oranges to produce about 2 cups of juice.

Pour the coconut water into a small saucepan and bring to a simmer. Remove from heat and add the orange zest and thyme. Let cool to room temperature, about 15 to 20 minutes. Discard the peel and thyme, and transfer the liquid to a blender. Add the agave, vanilla, camu berry powder, vodka, and blend to combine. Taste for sweetness: liquid should taste slightly over-sweet (once frozen, the sweetenss will be reduced). Depending on the sweetness of your fruit, add stevia as needed, about 8 to 12 drops. Blend once more, and pour into a shallow baking dish, such as a 9 x 9-inch pan. Place in the freezer until frozen, about 4 to 6 hours. When ready to serve, use the prongs of a fork to scrape up the granita into a "snow." Store the granita in the freezer, covered, where it will keep for several weeks.

> **SUPERFOOD TIP:** Another great way to infuse more flavor into granitas without effecting the overall nutrient density is through using flavored liquid stevia. Flavored stevias combine liquid stevia with various natural oils and extracts, such as lemon or orange. You can use this stevia in all kinds of healthy frozen treats for a sugar-free flavor boost.

KID SNACKS

Cue the fun! Super vibrant, simple, and full of friendly flavors, these "kid snacks" are all great ways to make sure that nourishing superfoods are a playful, welcome part of a child's snacking routine. Strawberries, mulberries, and chia seeds are just a few of the tried-and-true superfood favorties here. Of course, though these are wonderful snacks for kids, they're also adored by many of us big people who are just kids at heart, too.

 = FEATURED SUPERFOOD INGREDIENT

 BEAUTY   BONE STRENGTH   HEART HEALTH

 IMMUNITY   LOW CALORIE   PROTEIN

APPLE SANDWICHES

A friend once showed me an apple sandwich—an adorable (and delicious) idea which, it turns out, is nothing more than stacked apple slices spread with nut butter and granola. I was immediately enamored. So, here's a flexible take on this quick snack, now brought to a new level of nutrition and flavor with the simple addition of superfoods. You can use virtually any variety of whole, snack-friendly superfoods that you may have on hand, from fresh chopped berries to chia seeds to cacao nibs (and, if you're making this yummy snack with kids, better still, let them pick their favorite!). You can also use any kind of nut or seed butter you like, including any of the ones in this book. You can even sprinkle in some sweet spices such as cinnamon or superfood powders such as acai berry. Get creative!

MAKES ABOUT 4 SANDWICHES / 2 SERVINGS

1 apple, any variety, cored

2 tablespoons nut or seed butter

Whole superfoods, for sprinkling

Slice the apple into thin, ¼-inch thick slices. Spread the nut butter lightly on one side of a slice, then sprinkle it with the desired superfoods. Spread another slice of apple with nut butter and press the two slices together to make a sandwich. Repeat with the remaining slices and serve. Apple sandwiches will keep, wrapped and refrigerated, for 1 to 2 days.

GREAT COMBOS FOR APPLE SANDWICHES

- Cashew butter + fresh raspberries
- Almond butter + dried mulberries
- Coconut Butter (see page 114) + hemp seeds
- Tahini + dried goldenberries
- Power Seed Butter (see page 116) + dried goji berries

STRAWBERRY CHIA FRUIT STRIPS

You can feel great about giving this vitamin C–packed snack to a special kiddo, or enjoy it yourself. Not only is there no added sugar, unlike so many other recipes for fruit leather, but the addition of chia helps slow down the release of natural fruit sugars to make these fruit strips even more of a long-term energy snack. If you have some extra or overripe fruit in your kitchen that needs to be put to use, substitute away—this is a very flexible recipe.

A couple of tips: Since this recipe takes a bit of time in the oven, make the most of your efforts by doubling or even tripling the recipe. You can also use a tablespoon of liquid sweetener, such as yacon or agave syrup, in place of (or in addition to) the stevia, which will make the result a little more chewy.

MAKES 4 SERVINGS

2 cups strawberries, trimmed and chopped

2 cups bananas, peeled and chopped

8–10 drops liquid stevia*

1 tablespoon chia seeds

You may substitute with 2 tablespoons syrup or other sweetener of choice.

Preheat the oven to 150°F, or as low as your oven will go. Line a baking sheet with a silicone mat or parchment paper (silicone mat preferred).

Blend the strawberries to a liquid, then add the bananas and blend until smooth. Taste to determine the sweetness of the fruit and add stevia (and/or sweetener of choice) to heighten the flavor, blending to incorporate. Mix in the chia seeds by hand to distribute evenly.

Oven method: Since the oven will cook the edges of the fruit strips faster than the center, use the following method for the most even cooking: Pour a rectangular outline of mixture onto the silicone mat about 1 inch from the edges, then pour the remaining mixture into the rectangle to fill it. Use an offset spatula to carefully spread the mixture as evenly as possible across the entire surface of the mat. Jiggle the pan laterally to help smooth out the mixture. Place the pan in the oven and cook for 6 to 8 hours, until the mixture is slightly tacky to the touch with no wet pockets. (To keep the fruit

leather pliable and not crunchy like a chip, be sure not to overcook the mixture. Toward the end of cooking, check often, and if there are any sections that are done early, cut them off and remove them from the pan. Return the baking sheet to the oven.) Once cooked through, remove the pan from the oven and carefully peel the fruit off the mat. Use a pizza cutter or sharp knife to trim off the uneven border to make a rectangle, then cut the fruit leather into desired shapes.

Dehydrator method (preferred): Spread the mixture out onto several teflex dehydrator sheets. Dehydrate at 120°F, until a pliable leather has formed (about 8 to 10 hours, or overnight). Peel fruit away from the teflex and cut into desired shapes.

Variation: For an extra-condensed boost of antioxidants and vitamins, blend in your favorite superfruit powder, such as ½ teaspoon camu berry powder, 1 teaspoon maqui berry powder, or 1 tablespoon acai berry powder.

BLACKBERRY–VANILLA JIGGLE BLOCKS

Little fruit-infused jiggly cubes? Don't try to deny it: Jiggle blocks are just straight-up fun, and this recipe definitely raises the flavor and nutrition bar several notches above anything that ever came out of a boxed powder. Instead of gelatin, agar agar is the star here (see page 197 to learn more about this ingredient), and instead of sugar, a small amount of maple syrup is used to create a smooth texture (you can also use a few drops of liquid stevia to taste, if you prefer, but it will give the jiggle blocks a slightly firmer texture).

MAKES 8 SERVINGS

1 quart pure apple juice

3 cups frozen blackberries

¼ cup agar agar flakes

¼ cup maple syrup

2 teaspoons vanilla extract

Combine all the ingredients in a saucepan, whisk together, and bring to a boil. Reduce heat to medium-low and simmer for a full 5 minutes, stirring occasionally. Remove the mixture from heat and pour into a 9-inch square glass pan (or preferred container). Refrigerate the mixture until cool and fully set, about 4 hours. Cut the solidified mixture into small cubes and remove them from the container with a spatula, or simply spoon it out. The jiggle blocks will keep for several days, refrigerated.

> **SUPERFOOD TIP:** You can also use silicone ice cube trays as small jiggle molds (try the special shaped ones such as hearts or circles)—the jiggle bite will pop right out for serving in whatever shape you use.

BLUEBERRY–GINGER JIGGLE BLOCKS

Surprisingly, the taste of blueberries can be difficult to showcase without using flavor extracts. Here, combined with a hint of ginger, blueberries finally have a chance to glow in the spotlight. You can choose to leave the blueberries whole, for extra nutrition, or for a more refined presentation, you can strain them out before letting the jiggle blocks cool (most of the blueberries' juices and flavor are transferred into the mixture, in any case).

MAKES 8 SERVINGS

1 quart apple juice

2 cups frozen blueberries

¼ cup agar agar flakes

3 tablespoons maple syrup

2 inches fresh ginger root, peeled and sliced into 6 rounds

Combine all the ingredients in a saucepan, whisk them together, and bring to a boil. Reduce heat to medium-low and simmer for a full 5 minutes, stirring occasionally. Remove the mixture from heat and discard the ginger slices. Pour the mixture into a 9-inch square glass pan (or desired container). Refrigerate until cool and fully set, about 4 hours. Cut the mixture into small cubes and remove with a spatula, or simply spoon it out. The jiggle blocks keep for several days, refrigerated.

WHAT'S AGAR AGAR?

Agar agar is an ingredient used to create culinary magic. Most notably, it is used in classical Japanese cuisine to make jellies and puddings. Agar, a translucent white seaweed, is virtually flavorless and a superb vegetarian substitute for gelatin, which is made from animal skin, ligaments, and bones, etc. When agar is boiled with liquid, it melts down seamlessly, and when it is cool, the result is Jell-O-like. There are usually two ways to buy agar—in flakes or powder. For the best results, I recommend using the flake form, since powders can be inconsistent, and accurate measuring is important to create the right level of "jelly." On the surface of it, agar would appear to be an expensive ingredient, but very little of it is needed per recipe (about $1 to $2 worth). It's also an ingredient that will last for many years in the pantry.

WATERMELON PIZZA

This is the best (and healthiest) "pizza" ever! Kids LOVE making this fun recipe, and you may just find that you do too. Although the recipe calls for specific amounts and ingredients that go nicely together, the truth is it's highly flexible, and you can easily omit, swap, or add your kids' favorite fruits and ingredients. Or just put all the ingredients on the table to create a "pizza factory," and let the kids assemble their own pizza—a wonderful way to get children excited about vibrantly healthy food.

MAKES 4 PIZZAS / 4 SERVINGS

1 medium seedless watermelon

½ cup macadamia nuts, chopped

¼ cup dried goji berries

½ cup fresh blueberries, halved

2 kiwi, peeled and sliced thin

Handful fresh mint leaves, minced (optional)

Handful edible flower petals (optional)

Use the widest part of the watermelon to cut 4 1-inch-thick rounds. Each round will form the base of a "pizza." Decorate each round with the fruit, nut, and garnish toppings you like best. Use a chef's knife (adults only, please!) to cut each "pizza" into 8 wedges. Serve immediately. Watermelon Pizza will keep up to one day, covered and refrigerated.

Variation: Although Watermelon Pizza is delicious and fun for adults as well as kids, you might want to try a few of the following ingredients, which are more grown-up-friendly, and make a great party snack: shaved fennel, minced parsley, black pepper, sea salt, and a drizzle of olive oil. You can also add superfood cheeses to the mix. (See pages 100–106 for recipes.) They go surprisingly well with watermelon!

RAINBOW SUPERFRUIT POPSICLES

Of course you could make a single-color fruit, but why stop there when you can create a whole natural rainbow? Using frozen fruit allows you to get the effect quickly by making small batches of slushes that can be layered instantly—plus the pops will freeze faster, too.

MAKES ABOUT 10 POPSICLES / 10 SERVINGS

1 cup coconut water, divided

½ cup frozen blueberries

1 teaspoon maqui berry powder (optional)

1 cup apple juice, divided

½ cup frozen strawberries

1½ cup frozen mango chunks, divided

1 tablespoon dried goji berries

1 large orange, peeled and chopped

½ cup frozen pineapple

¼ teaspoon camu berry powder

Small handful baby spinach

5 drops liquid stevia per fruit base, to taste

Chill your popsicle molds by placing them in the freezer for a minimum of 20 minutes before beginning this recipe.

In a blender, puree ½ cup of the coconut water with the frozen blueberries and maqui berry powder. Note that each blended layer should be thick and very frosty—if not, add more frozen fruit. Taste for sweetness and add a little stevia to slightly oversweeten the fruit—about 5 drops should do the trick for each round. Blend the mixture once more. Divide it between 10 (or desired quantity) popsicle molds, filling each ⅕ high. Place the molds in the freezer while you prepare the next layer.

(Rinse the blender in between creating each of the 5 layers.)

Combine ½ cup of the apple juice and the frozen strawberries in the blender and puree. Blend in about 5 drops of stevia, or to taste. Fill each of the molds by another ⅕. Return molds to the freezer.

Puree the remaining ½ cup coconut water, ¾ cup of the frozen mango, and the goji berries together. Sweeten with stevia. Fill the molds another ⅕ and return to the freezer.

Next, puree the orange first to liquefy, then add the frozen pineapple and camu berry powder and blend. Sweeten with stevia. Fill the molds another ⅕ and return to the freezer.

Puree the remaining ½ cup of apple juice, the remaining ¾ cup mango, and the baby spinach. Sweeten with stevia. Fill the last ⅕ of the molds and add popsicle sticks. Return the molds to the freezer to freeze completely, about 1 hour.

QUICK COLOR GUIDE

Here's how to create a rainbow of popsicle colors :

Purple: ½ cup coconut water + ½ cup frozen blueberries + 1 teaspoon maqui berry powder

Red: ½ cup apple juice + ½ cup frozen strawberries

Orange: ½ cup coconut water + ¾ cup frozen mango chunks + 1 tablespoon goji berries

Yellow: 1 orange + ½ cup frozen pineapple chunks + ¼ teaspoon camu berry powder

Green: ½ cup apple juice + ¾ cup frozen mango chunks + handful baby spinach

SUPERFRUIT CHIA SQUEEZE

The only thing that's better than chia pudding is a fruity chia squeeze—a cross between a smoothie and baby food (there's something wildly addictive about sucking fruit-sweetened slippery chia seeds). Kids, and more than a few adults too, go crazy for these chia squeezes. Reusable squeeze pouches, which you can order online (see the Resource Guide on page 209), make for a mess-free portable experience. Or, of course, you can skip the "squeeze" altogether and just eat it with a spoon or a straw.

FILLS 4 4½-OUNCE SQUEEZE POUCHES / 4 SERVINGS

- 2 cups Superfruit Squeeze Base (recipe opposite)
- ¼ cup chia seeds
  Liquid stevia (optional)

In a shaker cup or mason jar with a lid, shake the squeeze base and chia seeds together. Taste the mixture and, depending on the fruit, boost the sweetness by mixing in a few drops of stevia (as the chia seeds thicken, sweetness will be slightly reduced). Refrigerate the mixture for a minimum of 30 minutes to allow the chia seeds to hydrate and thicken completely. Shake the mixture once, about 10 minutes after you put it in the fridge. The mixture should be thick, but easily sucked up through a straw—if it's too thick, mix in a tablespoon or two of juice to thin it slightly. Spoon the mixture into squeeze pouches, seal, and serve. Fruit squeezes will last several days, refrigerated.

SUPERFRUIT SQUEEZE BASE

You can easily substitute different types of juice, fresh fruit, and superfood powders to make an infinite number of base combos. Just combine your favorite choices with chia seeds, following the steps in the recipe opposite. Here are a few variations to try, pureeing any of the below combinations in a blender until smooth.

MAKES 2 CUPS

ACAI STRAWBERRY
1 cup apple juice + 2 cups strawberries
+ 2 tablespoons acai berry powder

GREEN BANANA
1¼ cups apple juice + 2 bananas + ¼ teaspoon
spirulina + small handful baby spinach

BLUEBERRY PEACH
1¼ cups coconut water + 1 cup chopped peaches
+ ½ cup blueberries + ¼ teaspoon ground
cinnamon

PINEAPPLE MANGO
1 cup pineapple juice + 1½ cups chopped mango
+ ¼ teaspoon camu berry powder

CARROT BANANA
1½ cups fresh carrot juice + 1 banana
+ 1 tablespoon goji berries

FRITZ'S GOOD DOG TREATS

It's fun to share the superfood love with your furry four-legged "kids"—they deserve it! Since I often boost the food bowl for Fritz, my German shepherd, with small amounts of superfoods such as kale, chia, and spirulina, it wasn't long before I started to make him some "good boy" special snacks, too. He truly loves them, and knowing that he's getting some extra, protective nutrition makes me feel good too.

MAKES ABOUT 1½ DOZEN SMALL TREATS

- 1 cup cooked quinoa
  ¼ cup peanut butter
- ¼ cup ground flaxseed powder
- ¼ cup parsley, minced
- 3 tablespoons dulse flakes

Preheat the oven to 350°F. Line one baking sheet with silicone mats or parchment paper.

In food processor, combine all the ingredients and process until a clumpy dough has formed. Stop the machine to test the consistency—dough should stick together very easily when pinched; if too dry, mix 1 more tablespoon of peanut butter. When a malleable consistency is achieved, form the dough into small balls, one tablespoon at a time, and use the back of a glass to flatten them directly on the prepared baking sheet. Bake the treats for 22 to 25 minutes until golden and mostly dried. Let them cool on the pan, and "serve" at room temperature. Stored in a sealed container, the dog treats will keep for up to 2 weeks.

FEEL-GOOD FACT: Each of the superfoods in these treats directly supports canine health: Quinoa is a great source of protein for strength; flaxseeds offer healthy fats that are important for joint health (and make fur extra glossy); dulse provides important minerals for overall vitality; and even the parsley can help promote fresher breath.

PART THREE

EXTRAS

SUPERFOOD SUBSTITUTION CHEAT SHEET

Whether you've run out of your favorite ingredient, don't feel like going to the store, or can't get a superfood quickly enough, here's a list of substitutes that can come in handy and save the day. Results may vary per recipe, but in most cases these quick subs will do the trick beautifully. Note that some substitutions are nonsuperfood ingredients and that substitutes can, of course, go both ways.

SUPERFOOD		SUBSTITUTION
Acai Powder	=	Maqui Berry Powder
Agave Syrup	=	Maple Syrup
Amaranth (whole)	=	Quinoa (whole)
Cacao Powder	=	Cocoa Powder
Camu Berry Powder	=	Omit from Recipe
Coconut Sugar	=	Xylitol, Date Sugar, or Cane Sugar
Spirulina or Chlorella Powder	=	Wheatgrass Powder
Dates	=	Raisins
Flaxseeds/Powder	=	Chia Seeds/Powder
Hempseeds	=	Sunflower Seeds
Kale	=	Swiss Chard
Mulberries (Dried)	=	Raisins
Quinoa Flakes	=	Rolled Oats*
Raspberries	=	Blackberries
Strawberries	=	Blueberries
Teff (whole)	=	Amaranth (whole)
Yacon Syrup	=	Maple Syrup

*Gluten-free rolled oats may be used.

CONVERSION CHART

NON-LIQUID INGREDIENTS (Weights of common ingredients in grams)

INGREDIENT	1 CUP	¾ CUP	⅔ CUP	½ CUP	⅓ CUP	¼ CUP	2 TBSP
Chia Seeds	163 g	122 g	108 g	81 g	54 g	41 g	20 g
Chopped fruits and vegetables	150 g	110 g	100 g	75 g	50 g	40 g	20 g
Dried goji berries	111 g	83 g	74 g	55 g	37 g	28 g	14 g
Nuts, chopped	150 g	110 g	100 g	75 g	50 g	40 g	20 g

Note: Non-liquid ingredients specified in American recipes by volume (if more than about 2 tablespoons or 1 fluid ounce) can be converted to weight with the table above. If you need to convert an ingredient that isn't in this table, the safest thing to do is to measure it with a traditional measuring cup and then weigh the results with a metric scale. In a pinch, you can use the volume conversion table below.

VOLUME CONVERSIONS
(USED FOR LIQUIDS)

CUSTOMARY QUANTITY	METRIC EQUIVALENT
1 teaspoon	5 mL
1 tablespoon or ½ fluid ounce	15 mL
¼ cup or 2 fluid ounces	60 mL
⅓ cup	80 mL
½ cup or 4 fluid ounces	120 mL
⅔ cup	160 mL
1 cup or 8 fluid ounces or ½ pint	250 mL
1½ cups or 12 fluid ounces	350 mL
2 cups or 1 pint or 16 fluid ounces	475 mL
3 cups or 1½ pints	700 mL

RESOURCES GUIDE

AMAZON
If you can't find it in the store, you can probably find it on Amazon.
Find here: Almost any shelf-stable ingredient or kitchen item you can't find in a store or elsewhere online, such as nutmilk bags, popsicle molds, reusable squeeze containers (for chia squeeze recipes), cheesecloth, and specialty powders, often at discounted prices. You can even get pantry items such as coconut yogurt, goji berries, or lucuma powder!
Visit: Amazon.com

BEAMING
Offers outstanding protein powder—my personal favorite for snack making (it tastes great and uses real vanilla bean for flavor).
Find here: Beaming Superfood Protein Blend
Visit: LiveBeaming.com

GRAINAISSANCE
Sells ready to bake-and-serve mochi made with organic brown rice. Also find this product in the refrigerated section of many natural food stores.
Find here: Mochi, and more
Visit: Grainaissance.com

MALDON SEA SALT
Sells excellent flaked sea salt. You can find their products in many grocery stores as well as online.
Find here: Flaked sea salt, smoked salt.
Visit: Maldonsalt.co.uk

MANITOBA HARVEST
Specializes in hemp foods, including pure hemp protein powder.
Find here: Hemp Pro 70˙ (a high-protein, water-soluble hemp protein powder that works incredibly well in snacks as an unflavored, unsweetened protein).
Visit: ManitobaHarvest.com

MAINE COAST SEA VEGETABLES
Provides a huge variety of certified organic, sustainably harvested seaweeds.
Find here: Dulse flakes, nori sheets, and more.
Visit: SeaVeg.com

NAVITAS NATURALS
Specializes in 100% organic superfoods and dried pantry items. Many of the specialty superfoods you will be able to find here, either on their online website, in health stores, or on the web.
Find here: Acai powder, cacao powder, camu berry powder, chia seeds, dried goji berries, dried goldenberries, flaxseed powder, hemp seeds, lucuma powder, maca powder, maqui berry powder, dried mulberries, raw cashews, and wheatgrass powder.
Visit: NavitasNaturals.com

NUNATURALS
Carries great stevia products.
Find here: Liquid, powdered, and even flavored stevia.
Visit: NuNaturals.com

NUTREX-HAWAII
Specializes in spirulina—the best I've come across in terms of quality. You can also find this brand in many health food stores.
Find here: Spirulina powder.
Visit: Nutrex-Hawaii.com

NUTS.COM
Carries an extensive selection of various nuts, seeds and dried fruits, often at excellent discount prices. Check out their large organic section and bulk items.
Find here: Just about any kind of nut, seed or dried fruit. Also carries specialty grains like buckwheat and amaranth, as well as flours like teff flour.
Visit: Nuts.com

SO DELICIOUS
Offers exceptional coconut yogurt and coconut milk, increasingly available in markets across North America.
Find here: Coconut Yogurt, boxed coconut milk, and more.
Visit: SoDeliciousDairyFree.com

VEGA
Offers some well-formulated protein powders (top-quality ingredients that assimilate very easily into juices and taste good).
Find here: Chlorella powder, Performance Protein Powder (vanilla recommended).
Visit: MyVega.com

BIBLIOGRAPHY

Aggarwal, Bharat B. PhD., and Debora Yost. *Healing Spices: How to Use 50 Everyday and Exotic Spices to Boost Health and Beat Disease*. New York: Sterling, 2011.

Alvarez-Suarez, José. "One-month strawberry-rich anthocyanin supplementation ameliorates cardiovascular risk, oxidative stress markers and platelet activation in humans." The Journal of Nutritional Biochemistry. March 2014.

"A randomized, double-blind, placebo-controlled clinical study of the general effects of a standardized Lycium barbarum (Goji) juice, GoChi." Journal of Alternative and Complementary Medicine. May 2008.

"Basic Report: 08123, Cereals, oats, instant, fortified, plain, prepared with water (boiling water added or microwaved)." Agricultural Research Service United States Department of Agriculture. November 2014.

"Basic Report: 12220, Seeds, flaxseed." Agricultural Research Service United States Department of Agriculture. November 2014.

Callaway, J. C. "Hempseed As A Nutritional Resource: An Overview." Euphytica. 2004.

Clum, Dr. Lauren, and Snyder, Dr. Mariza. *The Antioxidant Counter*. Berkley, CA: Ulysses Press, 2011.

Coates, Wayne. *Chia: The Complete Guide to the Ultimate Superfood*. New York: Sterling, 2012.

Di Perro, F, G. Rapacioli, E.A. Di Maio, G. Appendino, F. Franceschi, and S. Togni. "Comparative evaluation of the pain-relieving properties of a lecithinized formulation of curcumin (Meriva®), nimesulide, and acetaminophen." Journal of Pain Research. March 2013.

"Goji Berry (Wolfberry)." 2008–2013. ImmuneHealthScience.com. April 2014.

ISGA International Sprout Growers Association. Homepage. November 2014

Kaewkaen, P. "Mulberry Fruit Extract Protects against Memory Impairment and Hippocampal Damage in Animal Model of Vascular Dementia." Evidence-Based Complementary and Alternative Medicine. 2012.

Kalafati, Maria. "Ergogenic and Antioxidant Effects of Spirulina Supplementation in Humans." Medicine and Science in Sports and Exercise. January 2010.

Kilham, Christopher S. *The Whole Food Bible: How to Select & Prepare Safe, Healthful Foods*. Rochester, Vermont: Healing Arts Press, 1996.

Lewandowska, Anna. "Isothiocyanates May Chemically Detoxify Mutagenic Amines Formed in Heat Processed Meat." Food Chemistry. August 2014.

Ley, Beth M., Ph.D. *Maca: Adaptogen and Hormonal Regulator*. Detroit Lakes, MN: BL Publications, 2003.

"Maca." Memorial Sloan-Kettering Cancer Center. April 2013.

Maisto, Michelle. "Rediscovering Amaranth, The Aztec Superfood." Forbes. December 2011.

Meissner, H. O. "Use of Gelatinized Maca (Lepidium Peruvianum) in Early Postmenopausal Women." International Journal of Biomedical Science. June 2005.

Morgan, Helen C., and Kelly J. Moorhead. *Spirulina: Nature's Superfood*. Nutrex Inc. 1993.

Murray, Michael T., and Joseph E. Pizzorno. *The Encyclopedia of Healing Foods*. New York: Atria Books, 2005.

Pacheco-Palencia, Lisbeth. "Absorption and Biological Activity of Phytochemical-Rich Extracts from Açai (Euterpeoleracea Mart.) Pulp and Oil in Vitro." Journal of Agricultural and Food Chemistry. May 2008.

Preedy, Victor R., Ronald Ross Vatson, and Vinood B. Patel. *Nuts and Seeds in Health and Disease Prevention*. London: Academic Press. 2011.

"Phytochemicals and Cardiovascular Disease." American Heart Association, March 2014.

"Pomegranate Ellagitannin-Derived Compounds Exhibit Antiproliferative and Antiaromatase Activity in Breast Cancer Cells In vitro." American Association for Cancer Prevention Research. January 2010.

"Prostate Cancer, Nutrition, and Dietary Supplements." National Cancer Institute. October 2014.

Raloff, Janet. "Prescription Strength Chocolate, Revisited." ScienceNews. February 2006.

Rowe, Lynne. *Berry Boosters*. Michele Havlik/Minervaz. 2011.

Sansouci, Jenny. "Why Cut Out Peanuts?" Dr. Frank Lipman: The Voice of Sustainable Wellness. November 2013.

Schardt, David. "Chocolate and Brain Health." NutritionAction.com. Dec. 2013.

Scholey, AB. "Cocoa polyphenols enhance positive mood states but not cognitive performance: a randomized, placebo-controlled trial." Journal of Psychopharmacology. May 2013.

"Strawberries, blueberries can boost a woman's heart health: study." New York Daily News. January 2013.

"Strawberries Can Help Protect Skin From UVA Rays." Medical News Today. August 2012.

Somer, Elizabeth. *Food and Mood: Second Edition: The Complete Guide To Eating Well and Feeling Your Best.* New York: Henry Holt and Company. 1999.

Tate, Nick. "Eat Nuts, Lose Weight: Study." NewsmaxHealth. January 2014.

Teas, J. "Variability of iodine content in common commercially available edible seaweeds." Thyroid: Official Journal of the American Thyroid Association. October 2004.

University Saarland. "Preventive effect of plant sterols in Alzheimer's disease." ScienceDaily, October 2013.

"Vitamin C and Skin Health." Linus Pauling Institute at Oregon State University. September 2011.

Wang, S.Y., and A.W. Stretch. "Antioxidant capacity in cranberry is influenced by cultivar and storage temperature." Journal of Agricultural and Food Chemistry. February 2001.

Young, Shelley Redford, and Robert O. Young. *The pH Miracle: Balance Your Diet, Reclaim Your Health.* New York: Grand Central Life & Style. 2010.

Yuan, Yvonne V., Dawn E. Bone, and Meshell F. Carrington. "Antioxidant activity of dulse (Palmariapalmata) extract evaluated in vitro." Food Chemistry. September 2004.

Zavasta, Tonya. *Beautiful on Raw: Uncooked Creations.* Cordova, TN: BR Publishing. 2005.

Zelman, Kathleen M., MPH, RD, LD. "The Truth About Kale: Nutrition, Recipe Ideas, and More." WebMD. 2010.

ACKNOWLEDGMENTS

If there was a recipe for making a cookbook, it would go something like this: mix together one part following a dream, two parts dedication, and pour in heaps and heaps of teamwork. (Let cook for at least a year, stirring constantly.)

Thank you to the truly exceptional publishing team at Sterling—how lucky am I?! To my editor (and moreso dear friend) Jennifer Williams, thank you for your endless magic touches and behind-the-scenes encouragement. Also thank you to Christine Heun for all of your creative detail and eye for beauty; to Elizabeth Lindy for designing a cover that's gorgeous enough to eat; and to Kimberly Broderick for keeping all of us singing the "snacks" song in tune and on time.

To my agent Marilyn Allen, thank you for being a pillar of wisdom, navigation, and support.

To the superbly skilled Carolyn Pulvino, thank you for your lovely icon designs. And also thank you to all of the incredible people at Navitas Naturals for supporting me from the beginning as well sharing in the passion for superfoods and extraordinary health.

To my enthusiastic and ambitious recipe testers, thank you for contributing your time and your taste buds to ensure every recipe was just right. Your feedback proved invaluable! Thank you to Amanda Longstreth for your much-needed organization in this endeavor.

To my family and my friends, thank you for all of your unconditional love and encouragement throughout this whole process—I love you! Special thanks to my mom, for still devotedly looking after my writing after all these years. And to sweet Fritz, my four-legged family member, thank you for always making sure the kitchen floor is 100% free of crumbs.

To Oliver, thank you for your truly incredible photos that make every recipe come alive! Most of all, thank you for being side-by-side with me every step of the way, and for always bringing love into the kitchen. . . . The most important ingredient there is.

Finally, thank you to my readers, who have supported me through the years and been an inspiration for everything that I do. This book is dedicated to you!

ABOUT THE AUTHOR

Julie Morris is a Los Angeles-based natural food chef and advocate of whole, plant-based foods and superfoods. The bestselling author of *Superfood Smoothies* (Sterling 2013) and *Superfood Kitchen* (Sterling 2012), Julie has worked in the natural food industry for close to a decade as a recipe developer, writer, cooking show host, and spokesperson, and is the executive chef for Navitas Naturals, a fair trade company that specializes in 100% organic superfoods. Her mission is simple: to share recipes and nutrition tips that make a vibrantly healthy lifestyle both easy to achieve and delicious to follow. To learn more about Julie and superfoods visit juliemorris.net.

Photo: Oliver Barth

Photographer **Oliver Barth** was born and raised in Berlin, Germany. Barth is devoted to capturing the natural beauty of life in timeless images. He lives in Los Angeles, California. Visit Oliver Barth at ilovefoodphotography.com.

Photo: Steve Bonini